T0267179

A GARDENER'S GUIDE TO

PROPAGATION
TECHNIQUES

The essential guide to producing plants

A GARDENER'S GUIDE TO
PROPAGATION TECHNIQUES

The essential guide to producing plants

NIKKI BARKER

THE CROWOOD PRESS

First published in 2022 by
The Crowood Press Ltd
Ramsbury, Marlborough
Wiltshire SN8 2HR

enquiries@crowood.com
www.crowood.com

© Nikki Barker 2022

All rights reserved. No part of this publication may be reproduced or transmitted in any form or by any means, electronic or mechanical, including photocopy, recording, or any information storage and retrieval system, without permission in writing from the publishers.

British Library Cataloguing-in-Publication Data
A catalogue record for this book is available from the British Library.

ISBN 978 0 7198 4079 1

Cover: Blue Sunflower Creative

Typeset by Chennai Publishing Services
Printed and bound in India by Parksons Graphics

CONTENTS

1   Introduction to Plant Propagation   7

2   Propagation Systems, Environments and Materials   17

3   Seed Sowing   29

4   Softwood Cuttings   47

5   Semi-Ripe Cuttings   61

6   Hardwood Cuttings   75

7   Root Cuttings   83

8   Leaf, Leaf-Section and Petiole Cuttings   89

9   Layering   95

10   Division   101

11   Grafting and Budding   107

12   Bulb Propagation   119

13   Micropropagation   125

14   Pests, Diseases and Disorders   131

Index   144

CHAPTER 1

INTRODUCTION TO PLANT PROPAGATION

The Art of Propagation

Propagation is a skill that takes time and practice to master, and there is always something new to learn. Within each method there are plants that propagate quickly and easily, and plants that take longer and need more resources and equipment. Practising each method with the easier plants will give you confidence and improve your technique before moving on to more difficult subjects. This book aims to show you the techniques involved in each method and lists different plants that can be propagated by those methods, showing the level of difficulty for each plant. This will help you to select plants that you wish to propagate by the equipment and materials available to you, as well as your own skills.

What is Propagation?

Plant propagation is the method by which new plants are produced from seed or other parts of a plant. People have been propagating plants for centuries, and some of the techniques we use now have been refined from the way plants reproduce in their natural environment. Roman and Greek texts from over 2,500 years ago indicate that grafting, one of the more difficult methods of propagation, by which the growing plant is grafted on to another plant's rootstock, was being practised widely in orchards and fruit production. Weeds proliferating in garden borders are plants sexually reproducing and multiplying naturally, and when we sow seeds from packets, we are trying to provide the conditions that will promote maximum germination for the plants we want to grow. Other plants, such as *Lamium maculatum* and *Ajuga reptans* naturally use more than one method of propagation, and layer themselves by producing adventitious roots along their stems, which is why we consider them to be excellent climbing or ground-cover plants, as well as producing seed. Looking at how a plant reproduces in its natural environment can often give us clues about the best way to propagate from it.

So, people have been propagating plants, selecting desirable characteristics, for thousands of years, both for food production and to provide ornamental plants to make a pleasing environment. Propagation in the twenty-first century can have a high degree of mechanization, using mist systems, computer-controlled temperatures, ventilation and irrigation, but most propagation techniques can still be applied using less expensive equipment and resources, particularly if you wish to propagate smaller numbers of plants. One thing that hasn't changed much over the centuries is

Example of natural layering in *Ajuga*, *Lamium* and thyme.

Male squash flower – no swelling below flower.

that most of the actual propagation still needs to be done by a human being, so whilst the propagation environments become more computer controlled, artificial intelligence has yet to replace the skilled propagator.

Propagation – Sexual Plant Reproduction

Propagation from seed is the method by which plants sexually reproduce, through either being self-fertile or cross-fertilization. Dioecious plants, such as species in the genus *Ilex* (holly), have either male or female flowers on a single plant, so they require both a male and a female plant to produce seeds, which are inside the berries. Therefore, it is quite common to see a holly with no berries on next to one covered in berries – the plant with no berries is male, and the plant with berries is female. Monoecious plants, ranging from *Quercus* (oak) to cucurbits such as squashes and pumpkins, have both male and female flowers on a single plant, so can produce fruit or seed without having another plant nearby, although cross-pollination by another plant is still desirable for genetic diversity. However, all these plants may still require fertilization assistance, whether from pollinating insects, wind, mammals or, sometimes, a paintbrush to move pollen from a male flower to a female flower.

Plants have evolved a wide variety of methods to ensure that pollination takes place, and we see

Female squash flower with swelling below flower.

many of these examples in our gardens and the wider environment, often without noticing what is happening. Plants produce fragrance, nectar and brightly coloured flowers to attract insects, and many plants, including apples and pears, rely on insect pollination, for which bees are particularly important. Others such as *Salix* (willow) and *Betula* (birch) produce catkins, which release pollen on the wind. Flowering at the right time, to attract the right pollinator, is also important, as flowering too early or too late may result in low levels of fertilization. Some orchids have developed flowers that mimic both the appearance and scent of female wasps to attract male wasps, which try to mate with the flower – unsuccessfully – but transfer pollen very effectively!

Flower Parts for Sexual Reproduction in Flowering Plants (Angiosperms)

Pollination and fertilization are two different processes, but fertilization cannot happen without pollination taking place. Pollen is produced in the male organ of the plant, which is known as the stamen, and transferred to the female organ, known as the carpel. Fertilization then takes place, and part of the carpel becomes whatever type of fruit the plant produces, which contains the seed.

Some flowering plants are monocotyledons and can be identified by the parallel veining in the leaf and having no distinction between sepals and petals. They also tend to be non-woody plants, such as grasses, tulips and lilies. When the seed of a monocotyledon germinates, it only has one seed leaf.

Dicotyledons generally have distinct sepals and petals, and the leaves have a network of veins. They can be woody plants, as well as annuals and perennials, ranging from petunias to magnolias. When the seed of a dicotyledon germinates it has two seed leaves.

Hydrangea paniculate flower head.

Agapanthus seedlings, monocot seed leaves.

Seedling showing seed leaves and first true leaves on dicotyledon.

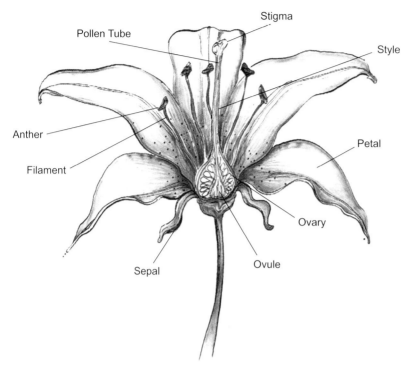

Cross-section showing flower parts for sexual reproduction.

Terms for flower parts

Carpel	The female reproductive part of the flower, composed of the stigma, style and ovary.
Stigma	This is the top of the style and is usually sticky to catch the pollen grains. This is where the pollen germinates.
Style	This holds the stigma in position to be most effective at catching pollen. When pollination has taken place, the pollen tubes grow down the style to the ovary.
Ovary	Surrounds the ovule, which contains the female gametes. The ovary has a thick wall that becomes part of the fruit after fertilization.
Stamen	The male reproductive part of the flower, composed of the anther, filament and pollen.
Anther	This is where pollen is produced.
Filament	The stalk that holds the anther in place.
Pollen	Pollen contains the male gamete(s) in angiosperms. (In gymnosperms these are produced in male cones.)
Receptacle	Holds the carpel and the stamen at the top of the flower stem.
Nectary	Where nectar is produced. Not all flowers produce nectar.
Corolla	Collective name for petals.
Calyx	Collective name for sepals.

Sexual Reproduction in Non-Flowering Plants (Gymnosperms)

Gymnosperm means 'naked seed' and this sub-king-dom of plants produce seeds but from cones rather than flowers, and the seeds are only partially enclosed. The most common type of plants in this group for propagation purposes is conifers. Whilst they are rarely propagated from seed commercially, conifers such as *Chamaecyparis lawsoniana* can often be found self-seeded in gardens. Conifers have male and female cones and are usually wind pollinated.

Cone of pine.

Propagation – Asexual Plant Reproduction

Vegetative reproduction uses different parts of the plant, stems, leaves, roots, offsets, to produce new plants and this is asexual reproduction – commonly known as vegetative propagation. Vegetative propagation is widely used commercially to grow large quantities of plants for the wider horticultural industry, from landscapers to garden centres. Vegetative propagation gives uniformity of production, with the cuttings being genetically identical to the parent plant (although mutations do occasionally occur) and can be large- or small-scale.

There are several methods of vegetative propagation, including cuttings, grafting, division and

Micropropagated orchid in flower.

micropropagation, and different species have different success rates with each method; so, commercially, the plant is produced using the most viable method. Orchids used to be an expensive plant to reproduce by traditional vegetative methods, but they are now commercially successfully reproduced using micropropagation, and are readily available almost all year round at reasonable prices.

Desirable characteristics that occur on a plant, such as variegation, can only be maintained by vegetative propagation, and it is by these methods that some of our most popular garden plants are produced for sale, ranging from *Euonymus fortunei* 'Emerald and Gold' to *Begonia rex*. Other methods of vegetative propagation confer other desirable characteristics, so fruit-tree cultivars can be grafted on to rootstocks that have dwarfing characteristics, as well as pest and disease resistance. This offers major advantages both for commercial orchard production, as well as the domestic garden.

The age of the plant material used for vegetative propagation is important, as juvenile material has higher hormone (auxin) levels, which increase the chances of successful rooting. Commercially, parent plants can be pruned to prevent flowering and encourage leaf growth, to provide more propagation material. Plants generally have higher hormone levels in spring, so cuttings taken at this time of year often root quickly and easily, whereas hardwood cuttings taken in winter are slower. However, there are still advantages to both methods, as softwood cuttings may require more environmental protection to help them to produce roots.

Propagation material should always be healthy, pest- and disease-free, and material should be selected from non-flowering stems to achieve high-percentage success rates. Collecting the material early in the day when it is turgid (full of water) and the temperature is cooler will also increase success rates.

Environmental Factors for Successful Propagation

Parts of a plant taken for vegetative propagation are called propagules. In the case of stem and leaf

The root environment

Growing medium	High-quality growing medium to allow good drainage but also moisture retention.
Water	Moisture levels should be stable, so that the growing medium does not dry out or become too wet.
Temperature	The temperature at the base of the cutting should be appropriate to the plant and method of propagation.
Air	There must be air in the growing medium to prevent waterlogging, which can lead to disease.
Nutrient	Nutrient levels should generally be low and increased once the root system is developed.

The aerial environment

Light	Adequate light is essential for photosynthesis to take place, but there should not be an excess of light, which can cause scorching. Shading can be used at times of year when excessive light levels may be an issue, and artificial lighting can be used when light levels are low.
Temperature	The temperature should be optimum to the plant and the type of cutting. A stable temperature is better than a fluctuating temperature in most protected environments, such as glasshouses. This can be achieved through ventilation and shading, as well as heating at cooler times of year.
Humidity	Higher humidity can reduce water loss through transpiration, so particularly for leafy propagules, the humidity around the cutting should be kept high. This can be achieved in a variety of ways, from automatic mist systems to putting a plastic bag over a pot of cuttings on the windowsill and hand misting them.
Air quality	The air needs to have carbon dioxide for photosynthesis and oxygen for transpiration. The air normally has the right balance, but sometimes increasing the humidity can reduce the amount of oxygen in the air, so a balance needs to be struck between humidity levels and ventilation for air quality.

cuttings, these have no roots, so the environment must provide all the needs of the propagule until it has produced its own root system. The propagule must be able to photosynthesize and respire, or it will die before roots start to form, but also water loss through transpiration needs to be reduced, as there is no root system to replace it. The environment should encourage the propagule to produce roots as quickly as possible. Most cuttings absorb water through the cut at the base of the stem but, after a few days, the cut calluses over, and this reduces the amount of water the cutting can absorb. Often cuttings can look fine for a few days, and then drop all their leaves and fail. The humidity levels need to be kept high at the point where the base of the cutting has callused over.

Advantages and Disadvantages of Seed and Cuttings

All methods of propagation have advantages and disadvantages, and some plants will grow from almost any method of propagation. *Buddleja davidii*, for example, will produce seed freely, which is why they are so successful on railway bridges and embankments. They also propagate easily from softwood, semi-ripe and hardwood cuttings. Therefore, the method you would use to propagate *Buddleja davidii* would be the method that suits the environment you can provide and is the most economically viable. For this reason, *Buddleja davidii* cultivars are often

Advantages and disadvantages of propagating from seed (sexual reproduction)

Availability	Some plants produce large quantities of seed, which are easily harvested. Vegetable seeds and many annual flowering plants are grown from seed, both commercially and domestically.
Cost	Easy availability of seed keeps the cost low, so large quantities of seed are comparatively cheap. Carrot seed packets often contain 2000 seeds, at low prices.
Reliable	Many plants grow readily from seed, whether direct in the ground, such as peas and beans, or started under protection. Seed purchased from reputable suppliers must undergo strict testing.
Genetic diversity	Plants grown from seed can give rise to genetic variations, which may be desirable in plant breeding.
Pest- and disease-free	Generally, seeds do not transmit pests, diseases or viruses in the same way that vegetative material can do. There are exceptions to this, such as tomato brown rugose fruit virus (ToBRFV).
Range	There are a wide range of seeds available, with some plant species having thousands of cultivars available from seed, especially vegetables.
Storage	Seeds can remain dormant for long periods of time; in the case of some seed this can be decades. This means that many seeds can be used as required and then stored into the next season. Other seed does need to be used within a shorter time frame, carrots being an example of seed that reduces in viability significantly after the first year.
Germination	Some seed is difficult to germinate, requiring specific conditions, which may include breaking dormancy mechanisms. For example, in the natural environment, some seeds need to pass through an animal gut to break dormancy, and those conditions need to be replicated for germination on a nursery or at home.
Viability	Some plants produce seed that has low germination rates as a ratio of seed sown. This can make it economically unviable to propagate from seed.
Variation	Most hybrids and plant cultivars will not produce seed that is true to type; therefore, for many popular garden plants, vegetative propagation is vital.
Commercial viability	Many hybrids and cultivars will only be true to type via vegetative propagation. Seed propagation may also be slower to produce saleable plants, and can take much longer before becoming mature enough to flower.

Advantages and disadvantages of vegetative propagation (asexual reproduction)

Clones	Vegetative propagation produces genetically identical material, so for cultivars and hybrids, this is the only reliable method of reproduction to maintain the same desirable characteristics of the parent plant.
Commercial viability	Many plants will be saleable more quickly if produced vegetatively, whether from cuttings or grafting. Grafted plants, such as wisteria, will produce flowers at a much younger age than if seed grown.
Uniformity	Batches of plants can be produced at the same time, which means that they will be ready for sale at the same time.
Normal reproduction method	Vegetative reproduction may be the plant's most successful natural method of reproduction, so replicating this is the easiest form of propagation. Strawberries are produced from runners both naturally and commercially. Bulbs are another example, where they produce bulblets or offsets naturally.
Preserving cultivars	Some plants, including many rose and fruit-tree cultivars, do not grow well on their own roots, so require grafting or budding on to more suitable rootstocks.

(continued overleaf)

continued

Pest and disease resilience	Cloned plants will all be equally susceptible to new pests, diseases or viruses. This can cause major environmental issues; for example, elm trees naturally reproduced from suckers, so did not have the genetic diversity to withstand Dutch elm disease.
Quantity	Whilst high volumes of vegetatively propagated plants are produced commercially, it requires more space and planning for the material to be available from the parent plants, in comparison to the volume of seeds that some plants can produce.
Labour	Propagation requires a skilled workforce to be able to produce the volume and uniformity of material.
Expense and environment	Generally, the environment required by vegetative propagation material is more expensive than seed sowing. Commercial glasshouses and propagation units are also high maintenance, as well as having ongoing utility costs.
Lack of diversity	Cloning plants does reduce the likelihood of genetic mutation or adaptation, which can result in new cultivars.

commercially propagated from hardwood cuttings, as this requires low input costs in the form of heating, water or other environmental protections, whilst still producing a saleable plant quickly. However, if you want to practice your technique for softwood or semi-ripe cuttings, *Buddleja davidii* is an easy plant to start with, and there is always plenty of material available.

As you can see from the last two Tables, the selection of the right method of propagation for a plant depends on a wide variety of environmental and economic factors, which apply both to commercial production and the domestic situation.

CHAPTER 2

PROPAGATION SYSTEMS, ENVIRONMENTS AND MATERIALS

Greenhouses, polytunnels and cold frames are all environments protected from the weather. This protection offers advantages for propagation, as the environments can be controlled, unlike the weather. Polytunnels and greenhouses can be heated to maintain constant air temperatures or controlled so that the heating only comes on when the temperature falls below a pre-set minimum, such as a frost-free setting. Heating large, open and non-insulated spaces like this can be expensive, so using a smaller, protected environment within a glasshouse or polytunnel is commonplace, both commercially and domestically. Greenhouse heaters for domestic use are readily available, with a range of thermostat controls, but the electric ones need a safe source in the greenhouse. Systems using either oil or electric are available for larger commercial glasshouses, as well as solar panel systems.

Setting up a smaller protected environment within a larger one offers versatility should the environment need changing from one crop to another. Some plants may be easily propagated without bottom heat, some root or germinate much more quickly with both bottom heat and high humidity, so the aerial environment around the propagules needs regulating. This could be in the form of a propagator lid in a domestic greenhouse or it could be a closed environment on a larger scale, created with metal or plastic hoops over a greenhouse bench, covered with clear plastic sheeting.

Maintaining humidity around cuttings helps to reduce water loss through transpiration. Softwood cuttings and more difficult-to-root subjects may require high levels of humidity over longer periods of time.

Ventilation is also an important consideration within a protected environment because it may become extremely hot, and air circulation becomes necessary. Opening doors and roof vents is usually sufficient in a domestic setting, but air fans can also be used in commercial environments to circulate air and cool the temperature.

Light, Shade and Temperature

Whilst plants require light to photosynthesize, propagules need protection from very high light and air temperature levels, as they have no root system to support them. Even when they are rooted, the root zone is not going to be able to support high transpiration levels. Shading can be painted on to domestic greenhouses, but shade netting can be used in both domestic and commercial settings. Shade netting can be purchased at differing shade densities, ranging from 10 to 80 per cent, although 20 per cent shading is suitable for most propagators' requirements. This will also cool down the area in the warmer months. Thermal screens are also used commercially for insulation in cooler months, and to provide shade for crops in the warmer months. These can be manually operated, or computer controlled with temperature and humidity ranges set at a pre-determined level, depending on crop requirements.

Humidity

Humidity can be monitored in commercial systems through the use of sensors, which can be regulated to the specific requirements of a particular crop. On a domestic scale, humidity thermometers are readily available.

Mist Systems

Mist systems use overhead irrigation nozzles that produce fine water droplets – the size of the droplet will vary depending on the nozzle size. The aim of mist units is for the water droplets to increase humidity and for the water to evaporate from the surface of the leaves on cuttings, thereby reducing transpiration.

Mist systems can be used on a wide range of vegetative propagation material, and is beneficial for difficult-to-root species, but will also speed up rooting of other subjects. Uniformity of rooting and increased rooting percentage are also benefits of using mist systems.

Commercial mist systems are usually computer controlled using environmental sensors to activate the mist frequency. The environmental sensors, such as electronic leaf sensors, monitor the humidity at the level of the cuttings. Light, temperature and humidity sensors are also used to control shading and screening.

Bottom heat is usually required with a mist system, as well as a well-drained propagation bed to quickly remove the excess water. Mist systems can be set up over benches or the beds can be on the floor, but there should be a sand bed underneath to allow for sharp drainage and capillary action to the growing media used for the cuttings.

Not all plants require a misting system – they are an expensive outlay but they can significantly speed up

Shade netting can provide different percentages of shade for different conditions and is used for protecting soft material from direct sunlight.

A mist unit provides optimum humidity to maximize rooting percentages, usually in conjunction with bottom heat.

rooting times and increase the percentage of cuttings that root successfully.

Closed and Open Mist

Closed mist is when an area within a glasshouse or polytunnel is covered by a plastic film using hoops or similar structures over the nozzles. The advantage of closed mist is that it can enable sections of a propagation unit to be used as needed, which means valuable resources such as water are not wasted.

Open mist systems can be used in polytunnels, glasshouses and outdoor beds, and are generally used on easier-to-root subjects – in the case of outdoor beds, they may not require bottom heat – and on high-volume material where entire areas can be used for one crop.

It is possible to install mist systems in domestic greenhouses, and domestic kits are available, although for small greenhouses it is unlikely to be cost-effective.

Different mist nozzles give varying droplet sizes.

Computerized pump systems provide the water pressure necessary for a mist unit.

Fog Systems

Fogging units use much smaller water droplets than mist units – generally less than 15 microns – and are able to keep the humidity in the unit at in excess of 95 per cent. They create a thin layer of moisture over the leaf, which reduces transpiration and cools excessive air temperatures. Another advantage of fogging units is that they do not saturate the growing medium as much as mist units, so heating costs for bottom heat are reduced. Having less water going to the rooting medium also reduces the chances of cuttings rotting or damping off, and fogging uses less water resources than mist. They are expensive systems to install, however, so may not be cost-effective for most species that root well in closed mist systems.

Heated Bench and Polythene

Many species do not require mist or fog for successful rooting, and the use of bottom heat under a low polythene cover with a thickness of 20–25 microns. Hoops and polythene can be used in a closed mist system on heated benches or heated floor space. Polythene can be clear or white, depending on the shading requirements of the crop and the time of year. This has the advantage of being cheaper than a mist unit and uses less water, although it may not be suitable for more difficult-to-root subjects.

In some cases, the polythene film can be laid directly over the cuttings, which creates condensation on the film, keeping the atmosphere directly above the cuttings humid. This method does require careful management to prevent damping off, and failed cuttings should be removed as soon as possible.

Soil-warming cables can be used to provide bottom heat for propagation.

Both these methods may also require shading over the polythene when used in spring and summer propagation cycles.

Sun Tunnels

Outdoor beds with a good-quality, well-drained growing medium can be used on easy to root, hardy, ornamental nursery stock subjects, such as deciduous berberis cultivars. Cuttings can be inserted direct into the beds that are covered using hoops and polythene sheeting or, alternatively, cutting trays on sand beds or directly on the floor can be covered with a low tunnel. The polythene is thicker than that used in closed mist (between 35 and 40 microns), which provides some protection from wind, but little frost protection. A mist irrigation line is attached to the ridge of the tunnel, which maintains some humidity, but usually additional irrigation may be needed direct to the growing medium. Shade netting may also be used over the polythene covering, particularly during the summer months to help prevent leaf scorch and drying out.

Low Tunnels

Low tunnels are essentially the same as sun tunnels but without the mist irrigation line inside the polythene. The growing medium must be moisture-retentive and well drained, and this type of environment is good for easy to root, hardy, ornamental nursery stock subjects that are required in volume. This method – and sun tunnels – is much

Low tunnels can be used as cloches for field growing or over sand beds for propagation.

lower cost than mist units or glasshouse facilities, and produce rooted cuttings that require much less weaning. It is used commercially mainly for semi-ripe cutting material, such as *Aucuba japonica* cultivars, *Cistus*, *Hypericum*, *Lavandula* and *Viburnum tinus*.

Materials

There is a wide range of equipment and materials that is available to aid propagation and increase your success rates, but the choices you make will depend on the plants you are propagating and the method of propagation. For the easiest seed sowing, half-hardy annuals, such as *Calendula officinalis* (English marigold) or *Nigella damascena* (love-in-a-mist), can be scattered on a border and left to germinate when the environmental conditions are suitable, but other seed may need to go through more complicated processes to break dormancy. As we master different methods and progress with our propagation techniques, the materials and equipment we require may become more sophisticated.

Growing Media

Even with little in the way of other equipment, one of the first things most methods of propagation need is a growing medium, which is the term for the material used to put the propagules or seeds in. Composts are growing media made up of different constituents, including coir (coconut fibre), composted bark, loam,

Cuttings rooting in a sun tunnel on a sand base.

sand, peat and grit. However, growing media could also be rockwool or wood shavings, both of which are used in hydroponic production.

For decades, the horticulture industry has used peat as the main constituent of most composts because it has all the properties necessary for successful propagation for most plants. It is slightly acidic, free-draining, has good moisture-retention properties and can have fertilizers added easily. It is also much lighter than soil-based composts, so it reduced transport costs and made manual handling much easier. The environmental impact of continued peat usage has meant that the industry has developed new recipes for growing media, with composted bark and coir becoming the main constituents in peat-free composts. They have similar properties to peat and can be used for propagating all but a very few specialist plants. Composted bark, coir and other constituents can be mixed to different ratios, depending on the

manufacturer and the purpose of the growing media. A peat-free compost mix for bedding plants may have slow-release fertilizers added that will last sixteen to eighteen weeks, and a finer grade of composted bark or coir, to allow for easy tray and pot filling, whilst hardy, ornamental, nursery stock mixes could have twelve- to eighteen-month slow-release fertilizers and a coarser grade of composted bark or coir.

There may need to be other ingredients added to composts, as well as fertilizers, to enable a specific plant crop to reach its potential. For professional composts these include controls for pests, such as vine weevil, and wetting agents for composts that require higher moisture retention properties, such as hanging basket and container composts, which are added to both professional grower and retail composts.

As the use of peat is being phased out, it will not be included in the types and properties of growing media constituents detailed.

Common growing media constituents and their properties

Coir	Coir pith is a waste product from coconut production. It has good water-retention capacity and can be use as part of a mix of ingredients in a compost or on its own. It is widely used as the growing medium in commercial strawberry production.

Composted Bark	Bark is matured or composted and used to produce compost with a good, free-draining structure. It has good moisture-retention properties and is a waste product of the forestry and timber industry. Small amounts of nitrogen may need to be added to the compost.

Loam	Loam is high-grade, sterilized agricultural soil and is not widely used in commercial composts but is still used in loam-based retail composts. It tends to be heavier than other constituents but does have good nutrient-retention capacity.

(continued overleaf)

continued

Vermiculite 	Vermiculite is a hydrated magnesium iron aluminium silicate (mica) mineral that is expanded through heating to high temperatures to produce the flakes used in propagation. It improves drainage, aeration and moisture retention, and is widely used in seed propagation.
Perlite 	Perlite is an expanded mineral aggregate that is sterile and contains no nutrients, but it is porous and holds water. It can be added to composts to improve aeration, drainage and moisture retention.
Sharp Sand 	Sometimes used in composts for taking cuttings as it improves drainage. Also adds weight to composts for mature plants, but it has become less common in commercial use.
Silver Sand 	Silver sand is sometimes used in propagation, particularly to mix small seeds in to aid even distribution.
Rockwool 	Rockwool is made from heating lava deposits to high temperatures and 'spinning' it to produce wool-like threads. It is commonly used in the building industry as an insulation material, but also widely used in hydroponic growing, particularly for tomato, pepper and cucumber crops. It drains very freely, is inert and sterile, which makes it ideal for the addition of hydroponic feeds.
Green Waste 	Composted green waste can be used as a main ingredient or part of a mix. Its properties vary depending on the original material, but there are several manufacturers producing composts that include green waste.

There are other materials that can be used in growing media, but many are not yet in wide commercial use, although research and trials are ongoing in many countries, particularly looking at how to use waste products for composts. Seaweed, moss and wood waste are three products that have potential for use as growing media, and research into these is ongoing.

Tools and Equipment

The tools you use for propagation will depend on the method you are using and your skills at propagation. Secateurs can be used for most types of cutting material but learning to use a knife can increase the quantity of material produced in each period. Cuttings from

Knives and secateurs

Propagation Knives 	Knives used for propagation need to be kept sharp, to produce a clean cut. There are specialist grafting knives, as well as dual purpose.
Grafting/Budding Knife 	These tend to have smaller blades and a bark lifter for easy insertion of the bud on to the rootstock.
Bypass Secateurs 	Secateurs are good for hardwood cuttings and lots of semi-ripe material, but may be too unwieldy for some softwood cuttings. Anvil secateurs are not suitable for use in propagation.
Scalpel 	Some exceptionally soft plant material may be best propagated using a scalpel.
Snips 	Useful on smaller, softer material such as lavender or penstemon.

plants such as *Hebe* or *Lavandula* can be produced more easily with a knife or snips, but practice first and use the tool that is safest and most comfortable for you. Carbon steel knives are preferable, as they are easier to keep sharp than stainless steel.

Keeping your tools sharp to give a clean cut will increase the percentage of propagules that root and makes the process safer for the propagator. Whilst practice is the best way of reducing the risk of cutting yourself, if you are going to have an accident with your propagation knife or tool, it is better to cut yourself with a sharp blade than a blunt one – the cut will heal quicker, and I say this from experience!

Cleaning your tools is important to prevent contamination from pests and diseases. Clean your tools down after every batch you propagate, using a good-quality disinfectant.

Labels and Labelling

Labels and labelling are keys to propagation, and are often overlooked. It is important to record the name of the plant you are propagating, as well as the date it was propagated. The date is not the date the cutting rooted or the seed germinated, but the date the cutting was taken or the seed sown. Knowing the exact time from sowing to germination or cutting to rooting will give information for making future production cycles more efficient. The quantity of cuttings taken, or seed sown, is also important information so that the success rates can be analysed.

Plastic labels can be re-used multiple times, and waterproof pens ensure that the information is not lost. Labels can be scrubbed clean after use.

Wooden labels and pencils are commonly used for domestic propagation.

There is a wide variety of labels available in different sizes to suit the size of container the propagules are in. Many labels are still made of plastic and can be written on in pencil or permanent marker, but they can be cleaned and re-used and last for several years. Wooden labels are recyclable, but generally are only good for one or two uses, and copper labels can only be used once, so these are better used for labelling permanent planting rather than propagation.

Containers, Cell Trays and Seed Trays

There is a wide variety of containers, modules and trays available for propagation, and the choice of these will depend on the propagation material or seeds you are sowing. The majority of these are still made from plastic, but most can be used many times if they are cleaned and sterilized after use. Most can also be recycled, but there can be issues finding a recycling point for the types of plastic used.

Cell trays, sometimes called module trays, are widely used in commercial horticulture because they make efficient use of compost, heating and water. Each cell will contain just enough compost for germination, and this means many propagules can be produced in a smaller area than by using traditional seed trays or pots. If heat is being provided, either at the base, heating the glasshouse or both, then fitting larger quantities of propagules in makes the process more cost-effective and energy-efficient. Different sized cell trays are also now available to the domestic user at most retail outlets and online. They are not single use, and may be cleaned and re-used for many years.

Bio-degradable cell trays, blocks and pots are also available. The bio-degradable blocks are used commercially for some bedding plant production, and the use of bio-degradable and recyclable cell trays and pots for the saleable product going to retail outlets is becoming more common in bedding plant and nursery stock production.

Module trays come in a range of sizes to suit the seed or material to be propagated. They can be cleaned and reused multiple times.

Expanding pellets of coir are easy to store, and then soaked when required for use.

Propagators and Propagation Environments

There are many different sized propagators available for domestic use, and these can be used to produce a significant quantity of plants. Choose the size that is suitable for the space and environment you have available to you. Consider whether you have electricity available for a heated propagator, as bottom heat can make a significant difference to germination and rooting speeds, as well as the relative humidity inside the propagator. Some have thermostat controls so that you can adjust the bottom heat temperature, while others are a set temperature, usually between 16 and 18°C.

If you have a large enough greenhouse, you can make your own heated propagation environment using soil-warming cables or a heated mat, and larger versions of these are generally used commercially. Heated mats are laid on the bench. Soil-warming cables are usually embedded in sand or polystyrene to spread the heat out evenly. They usually have thermostat controls that cover a wider range of temperatures than domestic propagators.

Capillary matting is a material that absorbs and releases water by capillary action to the soil in the propagation trays, so it is used over the heated mat or cables to provide moisture to the propagules. Keeping the capillary mat watered, rather than overhead watering, can prevent under- and overwatering, and in some cases fungal diseases.

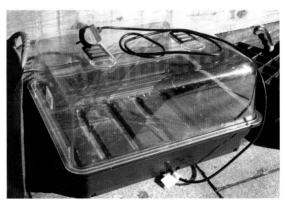

Domestic propagators are available with and without thermostats, and can make a considerable difference to success in home propagation.

Heated cables can be a laid in a sand bed as a cheaper alternative to a heated propagator.

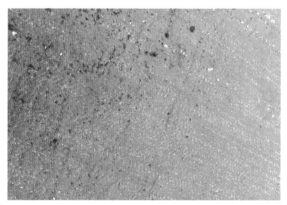

Capillary matting absorbs moisture and retains it, providing moisture to roots, reducing overwatering.

Watering

Domestically, a watering can with a fine rose can be used to water the propagules, and this will also provide some humidity around the leaf zone. Alternatively, cell and seed trays can be placed in a gravel tray, and the water will be absorbed by capillary action to wet the compost or growing media being used. Mist sprayers can be used to maintain the humidity around propagules, whilst avoiding overwatering the compost.

Commercial propagation units may have computer-controlled irrigation methods, which could range from mist systems to drippers wetting the capillary matting on benches, which are particularly useful for crops that dislike overhead watering.

General Equipment

There are other items that need to be considered for propagation. Maximum/minimum thermometers will give you a good idea of the temperature fluctuations around your propagation environment and may indicate how much heating or ventilation you need for a crop.

Gloves can provide protection from plants that cause skin irritation and protects cuts on the hands from possible sources of infection. It is important to remember that the gloves need to be thin enough for the knife or secateurs to be operated safely and not to impede dexterity. Latex and nitrile gloves can be recycled and there are both domestic and commercial schemes for this, which may incur a cost. Gloves contaminated with hazardous waste cannot currently be recycled.

A workspace where the propagation can take place is important to consider. Having a dedicated propagation area where the propagules, particularly in the case of softwood cuttings, are produced and quickly moved to the propagation environment, such as a mist unit, will result in fewer failures. A solid table or workbench that can be cleaned down after use is ideal.

Top Tip: Fill your cell trays or seed trays up before you start producing the propagation material. The cuttings can then be inserted quickly in batches, which means that they are less likely to dry out and become unviable.

Grafting plants will require items that other methods of propagation do not, so grafting ties or bands, grafting tape and grafting wax are needed for different grafting techniques. It is a good idea to practice grafting on easily available material before investing in the specialist equipment needed. *Salix* (willow) and *Cornus alba* (dogwood) make good practice plants, as you can mix different stem colours to perfect your technique and practice tying, and then dispose of them.

A workbench that is easily cleaned, with space for all the necessary equipment, makes propagation easier.

Chemicals and Biological Controls

Controlling pests and diseases in the propagation process can be done by using fungicides and pesticides, but the crucial element is maintaining a hygienic and suitable propagation environment. All equipment should be clean and preferably sterilized, the compost should not be waterlogged, and the humidity and ventilation should be controlled to reduce susceptibility to fungal diseases. Plant debris from leaves that fall during the propagation process should be removed, as should any leaf material that starts to die off or propagules that are obviously failing.

Chemical controls in a commercial environment can be applied by a licensed operator, and there are pesticides and fungicides available to the amateur gardener that have some effect on pests and diseases. Biological controls are becoming more widely used as an important part of integrated pest management (IPM) systems. They are organisms that control the pest through a variety of methods, such as predation, parasitism or by being a pathogen. The advantage of biological controls is the reduction in pesticide and other chemical usage, and the controls are targeted. Many are available to the amateur as well as the professional horticulturist. Using chemical or biological controls has a cost implication and is not a substitute for managing the propagation environment; however, there will always be occasions when pests or diseases occur. The most common types of pest and disease and their controls will be addressed in Chapter 14.

Hormone-Rooting Agents

Hormone-rooting agents, in either powder or liquid form, can speed up root production and make difficult-to-propagate plants viable by vegetative methods. The most commonly used commercially contain indole-3-butyric acid (IBA) in percentages ranging from 0.1 per cent to 2 per cent and are recommended for use according to the manufacturers' instructions, with detailed lists of which strength to use on which plant available as data sheets. Domestic users can also purchase hormone-rooting agents containing IBA, at the lower concentrations.

CHAPTER 3

SEED SOWING

Growing from seed can be the easiest way to propagate plants and is often where we all start. There is a wide range of seeds to choose from and it is generally cheaper than buying plants for the garden. On a commercial scale, high volumes can be achieved, often without the high levels of protected environments required for cuttings, grafting and micropropagation.

Seed Treatments

Many seeds require 'treatments' to trigger germination. Essentially these treatments usually replicate conditions that would occur in the plant's natural environment, which provide the seed with the best chance of successful germination, growth, flowering and sexual reproduction. The basic treatments are:

- Stratification – a warm or cold period.
- Scarification – a physical action on the seed that breaks down the outer layer.
- Soaking the seed – which softens the outer layer.
- Light or dark – some seeds require one or the other to trigger germination.
- Fire and smoke – some seeds require bush fires or heath fires to break seed dormancy.

In the natural environment, the cold period is provided by winter temperatures, the hot period by spring or summer temperatures, the physical action may be provided by passing through an animal gut, for example, and the soaking may be from spring rains.

Cold stratification can be replicated using a fridge, cold store, a cold shed or similar. The temperatures usually need to be around 1–5°C for the cold stratification, and warm stratification can be provided by a heated propagator, generally between 18 and 24°C. Seeds requiring cold stratification can be placed in airtight containers, with slightly moist compost or vermiculite, and left in cold storage for a few days to several weeks, depending on the individual species. If the seed starts to germinate while in cold storage, then remove it and sow it straight away.

Warm stratification can usually be replicated by the use of bottom heat, either with soil-warming cable on a propagation bench or individually heated propagators. For many seeds, the use of bottom heat increases the percentage germination rate considerably, and also the speed of germination, which makes up for the cost of the protected environment required. A few plants, such as *Styrax* and *Fraxinus excelsior*, require a period of warm stratification followed by cold stratification, so may need to be left through a summer and winter after seed ripening before they will germinate naturally.

Scarification can be replicated using an abrasive material like sandpaper or by nicking the seed with a knife, which breaks down the outer coat on the seed allowing moisture to penetrate. Soaking seeds in warm water for up a few hours, or up to two days depending on species, also breaks down the outer seed coat; the seed should be sown straight afterwards so that they don't dry out again.

Many of the more commonly propagated seeds will germinate below the soil or compost, or on top, but a few require either light or dark, and will not germinate without it. *Digitalis*, *Platycodon* and *Betula* all require light to germinate, and others such as *Begonia semperflorens* and *Nicotiana* prefer light to darkness. This is where using vermiculite is useful, as small, light-sensitive seeds can be sown with a light layer of vermiculite on top, which allows light to travel a short distance as far as the seed, but also provides warmth and nutrient-retention capacity. Seeds that need darkness to germinate include hellebores, cyclamen and delphiniums.

Most commercial seeds are selected and produced with ease of successful germination as one of the main factors, so the requirement for dormancy-breaking is not common, unless you are collecting your own seed or producing species that have dormancy factors, e.g. tree species for forestry planting.

Methods of Seed Sowing

The method used to sow seed will be dependent on the requirements for maximizing germination. As previously stated, some seeds need stratification, others need bottom heat and this varies not just from genus to genus, but different species within a genus may have completely different requirements. Another factor that is frequently overlooked in the domestic setting is seed size. Seeds range from very large, *Lodoicea maldvica* has seed that can weigh up to 18 kg, to seed from epiphytic orchids which are 0.2 mm in length and comparable to a speck of dust in weight. These are not the types of seed that are commonly sown on production nurseries or by the home gardener, but there is still a significant difference between the size of a broad bean seed (large) and the seed of *Lobelia* 'Crystal Palace' (tiny). Seeds that cannot be picked up individually by hand are considered small,

Commonly sown tree seeds that require dormancy to be broken

Seed	Environment Requirement	Difficulty Level
Betula pendula	Cold period – approximately 4 weeks	Medium
Corylus avellana	Cold period – 12–16 weeks	Medium
Crataegus monogyna	4–8 weeks warm period followed by 12–16 weeks cold period	Difficult – may require other dormancy breakers such as scarification.
Cupressus macrocarpa	4 weeks cold period	Easy
Euonymus europaeus	8–12 weeks warm period followed by 8–12 weeks cold period	Difficult – may require other dormancy breakers such as scarification
Fagus sylvatica	4–18 weeks cold period	Easy
Fraxinus excelsior	8–12 weeks warm period followed by 8–12 weeks cold period	Medium – seed may also require soaking prior to germination
Ilex aquifolium	20–40 weeks warm period followed by 16–24 weeks cold period	Difficult
Sorbus aucuparia	2 weeks warm period followed by 14–16 weeks cold period	Easy

with seeds like lettuce, tomato, zonal geraniums and tagetes medium, and beans, pumpkins and squashes are large seeds.

As a general rule of thumb, sow the seed three times the depth of its size, but this doesn't work for every seed, and knowledge of individual species' requirements is essential. Large- and intermediate-sized seed are easy to sow individually in cell trays, or placed individually at intervals in a seed tray. This makes it easy to sow the correct quantity, and also to have the necessary space between them when they germinate. Tiny seed is often sold commercially by weight, with a specific quantity of seeds per gram. These very small seeds are usually mixed with silver sand or vermiculite when sown to ensure even distribution over the cell or seed tray. Commercial plug-plant producers will also use mechanized seed-sowing to ensure that the correct weight or quantity of seed is sown in each cell of a module tray. Other seeds, such as coriander or flat leaf parsley and micro salads, are sown in groups of seed, even though the seed

Sizes of commonly sown seeds

Small Seed	Intermediate Seed	Large Seed
Begonia	Antirrhinum	Courgettes
Brassica	Beetroot	Cucumber
Limnanthes	Cerinthe	Helianthus
Lobelia	Escholtzia	Squashes
Nicotiana	Gazania	
Papaver	Geranium	
	Lathryrus	
	Lettuce	
	Nasturtium	
	Phacelia	
	Spinach	
	Tomato	

is larger, to be sold as cut and come again pot herbs, e.g. the pots of culinary herbs available in supermarkets for use in the kitchen.

Seed size will also inform the choice of seed tray or module tray size. Some tree seed may need to go in deep root-trainer cells, which also work well for sweet peas and other legumes.

Outdoor Seed Sowing

A wide range of seed can be sown outdoors directly into the ground. Many hardy annuals and vegetables can be sown straight into a prepared seed bed. Commercially, forestry trees, hedging and rootstocks can be field-grown from seed, providing good-quality, hardy stock that can be 'lifted' at the required size or age.

Preparing a seed bed can be done by hand on a small scale, but for commercial seed beds, machinery is used to cultivate the soil. The seed bed should be in a sheltered site, or artificial windbreaks can be used, if necessary. The soil should be weed-free and cultivated to a depth of between 10 and 20 cm (4 and 8 in), depending on soil type, ensuring that stones and clods of soil are removed or broken up, and that the soil is well drained. When cultivating, it is important not to

'Cut and come again' pot of parsley.

create a soil pan, particularly on clay soils. A soil pan occurs when the soil particles are compacted together, often just below the top-soil layer, and forms a layer that plant roots cannot penetrate and that prevents water draining freely. Mechanical cultivation over a period of years to the same depth will create a soil pan. When cultivating by hand, use a fork to loosen any compaction that may cause a pan, and aerate the soil. The bed can then be raked to remove any stones or lumps of soil, and the tilth on the surface of the soil should have a fine crumb structure, of between 1 and 3 mm.

Some seeds, e.g. green manures and grass seed, can be 'broadcast' sown over the seed bed. This involves scattering the seed over a designated area, either by hand or by machinery.

Drill sowing 'V'.

Drill sowing is when a shallow 'V'-shaped row is marked out using a string line and the drill is made using the edge of a hoe or tool handle, usually to a depth of between 0.5 and 2 cm $\left(\frac{1}{5} \text{ and } \frac{4}{5} \text{ in}\right)$, depending on the seed. The seed is then trickled into the drill, and the soil drawn back over the seeds. Carrots, spring onions, lettuce and many other vegetables can be sown using this method, and then thinned out as they germinate.

A wide, flat-bottomed drill can be made for seeds such as peas and beans. Use the hoe to create a deeper, wider drill by dragging the hoe toward you along the

Flat-bottomed drill.

Seed bed preparation.

string line. The depth will depend on the seed being sown, but is generally about 5 and 7.5 cm (2–3 in) deep. The seeds are then placed individually at the required distance from each other, and the soil drawn back over and lightly compacted using the hoe.

Station sowing is similar to a flat-bottomed drill, but three or four seeds are placed at each interval. This is useful for seeds that have erratic germination, such as parsnips, and if more germinate than expected, then the weaker ones can be thinned out from each 'station', leaving the strongest seedling to grow on.

Depending on your requirements, seeds can also simply be sown individually in a prepared area. Squashes are a good example, as the seed is very large and you may not require more than two or three plants, but they will cover a large area.

Seeds commonly sown direct outdoors

Broadcast	Drill	Flat-Bottomed Drill or Station Sowing	Individual Sowing
Grass seed	Beetroot	Beetroot	Beans – climbing
Wild flower seed mixes	Carrots	Broad beans	Beans – French
	Lettuce	Parsnips	Beans – runner
	Spinach	Peas	Potato tubers

Sowing Seeds in a Protected Environment

Sowing seeds in a protected, indoor environment generally means more even and faster germination, but has added expense in comparison to outdoor sowing. However, many plants would not be commercially viable if they were not sown in a protected environment, including most half-hardy annuals.

A protected environment can range from a cold frame to a heated propagator to a mist unit – all help break dormancy by providing extra protection, and usually extra heat at the root environment. Many seeds benefit from bottom heat and higher air temperatures, which can be provided by the different protected environments discussed in Chapter 2. In a domestic setting, seed or cell trays can be used in heated propagators, although even unheated propagators will provide some benefits, as the compost will provide some protection and the watering will be controlled. Commercially, heated benches and capillary matting provide controlled conditions for germination, and the benches can be covered with clear polythene over hoops, if required.

Sowing Seed Indoors – Cell Trays and Seed Trays

Step 1: Fill cell tray or seed tray with good-quality seed compost.

Step 2: Firm down compost.

Step 3: Sow the seed to the required depth.

Step 4: Cover with vermiculite, if required.

Step 5: Water from the bottom if possible (notice how the vermiculite turns darker as the water rises). Place in a protected environment.

Sowing Very Small Seed

Step 1: Fill cell tray or seed tray with good-quality seed compost.

Step 2: Firm down compost.

Step 3: Mix seed with silver sand or vermiculite.

Step 4: Cover the surface with the seed mix.

Step 5: Water from bottom, if possible, to prevent the seed being washed into clumps. Place in a protected environment.

Aftercare and Potting On

Field or outdoor, direct-sown seedlings are usually left *in situ* for either their entire lifespan – carrots, beetroot, peas, parsnips – or for several months/years until they are of the required size for lifting and transplanting. The areas should be kept weed-free and watered as necessary during periods of drought or excessive heat.

Seedlings in protected environments need careful management of the water levels around the root zone, as the compost needs to be moist but drain freely, because seeds need air as well as moisture for germination to take place. Bottom heat obviously causes evaporation of the water, so it can be easy for the compost to dry out. If the bench is also covered, the evaporation will increase humidity under the covered area, which can be a problem after germination, as it provides ideal conditions for diseases, such as botrytis, which cause damping off and death of the seedlings. The areas should be checked regularly for signs of germination and, once germination has taken place, covers can be removed for periods of time to ventilate the aerial environment around the seedlings.

Seeds sown in a protected environment will need pricking out and potting on much more quickly. Seed composts are generally low in nutrients, as high-nutrient content can inhibit germination and root production, so once seedlings have germinated, they are potted on into a compost with a higher nutrient content to promote growth. Seedlings are pricked and potted on when they have developed their first 'true' leaves, which are the first pair of leaves to develop after the seed leaves. Cell trays have distinct advantages when pricking out, as you are less likely to damage the stem or root of the seedling and you can pot on with very little contact with the seedling. Pricking out seedlings from seed trays can mean breaking roots and holding the stems to separate seedlings, which can retard their growth once potted on.

Ornamental Plants to Grow from Seed

The information provided in the difficulty rating is subjective, and inclusion in the list below doesn't mean that seed is the best way to propagate a particular plant, but that it can be propagated by seed. Some plants have cultivars that come true from seed, which is why the term cultivar has been included for some species and not others. Pre-treated seed will not necessarily require dormancy to be broken, so follow the instructions provided by the seed house from which the seeds are purchased. Some plants that are classed as difficult will be easier if pre-treated seed is purchased.

The cold stratification period can often be achieved by sowing the seeds in the autumn and, naturally, cold winter temperatures will provide the cold period, followed by warmer spring temperatures breaking dormancy.

Key to difficulty rating

Easy	Germinates easily, high-percentage germination, requires little or no dormancy treatments, requires little or no protected environments
Medium	May require some dormancy treatments and/or enhanced environment, such as bottom heat for good germination rates
Difficult	Requires dormancy treatments and/or protected environments, erratic and/or long germination times

Ornamental plants to grow from seed and their difficulty rating

Plant	Propagation Requirements
Abies fraseri	4–12 weeks stratification required, use fresh seed under 1 year old
Abies koreana	4–12 weeks stratification required, use fresh seed under 1 year old
Abies nordmaniana	4–12 weeks stratification required, use fresh seed under 1 year old
Abutilon cultivars	Germinate faster with bottom heat
Acacia dealbata	Soak in boiling water for 1–2 days prior to sowing, can also be scarified (nick the seed). Prefer bottom heat, usually beneficial
Acanthus mollis	Can be sown in cold frame or outdoor bed. Quicker germination with bottom heat
Acanthus spinosus	Can be sown in cold frame or outdoor bed. Quicker germination with bottom heat
Acer campestre	8 weeks warm period (15°C) followed by 20–24 weeks cold period (4°C)
Acer capillipes	Soak in hot water for 24 hours, stratification of 17–20 weeks warm period (20°C), followed by 16–18 weeks cold period (4°C)
Acer davidii	Soak in hot water for 24 hours, stratification of 17–20 weeks warm period (20°C), followed by 16–18 weeks cold period (4°C)
Acer griseum	Soak in hot water for 24 hours, stratification of 17–20 weeks warm period (20°C), followed by 16–18 weeks cold period (4°C)
Acer japonicum	Soak in hot water for 24 hours, stratification of 8 weeks warm period (20°C), followed by 8 weeks cold period (4°C)
Acer negundo	Soak in hot water for 24 hours, stratification of 8 weeks warm period (20°C), followed by 8 weeks cold period (4°C)
Acer palmatum	Soak in warm water for 24 hours, stratification of 8–12 weeks cold period (4°C), followed by 8–12 weeks warm period (4°–8°C)
Acer campestre	8 weeks warm period (15°C) followed by 8 weeks cold period (4°C)
Acer pseudoplatanus	12 weeks cold period (4°C)
Achillea filipendulina	Germinate well with bottom heat, leave seeds uncovered, sow on to surface
Achillea millefolium	Germinate well with bottom heat, leave seeds uncovered, sow on to surface
Aconitum carmichaelii	Require a cold period of 3–4 weeks at 4°C – keep the seed moist during stratification
Aconitum napellus	Require a cold period of 3–4 weeks at 4°C – keep the seed moist during stratification
Actaea simplex Atropurpurea Group cultivars	Cold stratification for 6–8 weeks (4°C) followed by warm period (10–15°C). Sow seed on surface and do not cover. Germination can be erratic
Actinidia kolomikta	Cold period of 10–12 weeks, then sow with bottom heat. Germination can be 8–12 weeks
Aesculus hippocastanum	Sow fresh as soon as the seeds are ripe; they do not store well
Agapanthus africanus	Store seed overwinter in a cool, dry place and sow in spring. Germination is quicker with bottom heat
Agapanthus campanulatus	Store seed overwinter in a cool, dry place and sow in spring. Germination is quicker with bottom heat
Agastache foeniculum	Germinate faster with bottom heat
Agastache 'Tango'	Germinate faster with bottom heat
Ageratum houstonianum and cultivars	Germinate faster with bottom heat
Akebia quinate	6–8 weeks cold period (4°C) followed by soaking for 24 hours in warm water. Sow on surface, bottom heat usually required
Alcea rosea and cultivars	Can be sown in cold frame or outdoor bed. Quicker germination with bottom heat
Alchemilla mollis	Can be sown in cold frame or outdoor bed. Quicker germination with bottom heat. Sow seeds on surface of compost or soil

(continued overleaf)

continued

Plant	Propagation Requirements
Allium schoenoprasum	Can be sown in cold frame or outdoor bed. Quicker germination with bottom heat
Allium tuberosum	Can be sown in cold frame or outdoor bed. Quicker germination with bottom heat
Alnus cordata	4–6 weeks cold period at 4°C
Alnus glutinosa	4–6 weeks cold period at 4°C
Alnus incana	4–6 weeks cold period at 4°C
Amelanchier canadensis	12–24 weeks cold period at 2–4°C – do not allow the seed to dry out
Amelanchier lamarckii	12–24 weeks cold period at 2–4°C – do not allow the seed to dry out
Anaphalis triplinervis	Can be sown in cold frame or outdoor bed. Quicker germination with bottom heat
Anemanthele lessoniana	Sow uncovered or light vermiculite covering. Bottom heat of 18–20°C required, germination will take place over several weeks
Anemone coronaria cultivars	Bottom heat of 18–20°C, germination erratic over several months
Angelica gigas	2–3 weeks cold period (4°C) then sow with bottom heat of 18–20°C
Angelonia angustifolia cultivars	Germination faster with bottom heat
Antirrhinum majus	Can be sown in cold frame or outdoor bed. Quicker germination with bottom heat
Antirrhinum majus	Cultivars can be sown in cold frame or outdoor bed. Quicker germination with bottom heat
Aquilegia vulgaris and cultivars	Can be sown in cold frame or outdoor bed. Quicker germination with bottom heat, germination can still be erratic
Arabis caucasica and cultivars	Can be sown in cold frame or outdoor bed. Quicker germination with bottom heat, germination can still be erratic
Aralia elata	Soak for 24 hours, 12–14 weeks cold period (4°C)
Araucaria araucana	Sow seed on surface, requires 15°C bottom heat, germination takes several weeks
Arbutus unedo	10–14 weeks cold period (4°C) then soak seed for 5–7 days in warm water prior to sowing
Armeria maritima	Can be sown in cold frame or outdoor bed. Quicker germination with bottom heat
Aronia melanocarpa	12 weeks cold period (4°C)
Artemisia aborescens	Can be sown in cold frame or outdoor bed. Quicker germination with bottom heat
Aruncus dioicus	Can be sown in cold frame or outdoor bed. Quicker germination with bottom heat, germination can still be erratic
Asplenium scolopendrium	Sow spores on to sterilized compost, cover with clear polythene film straight after sowing. Require light but not direct sunlight, cool conditions. Germination takes several weeks
Astrantia major	4–6 weeks cold period, seed must be kept moist. Bottom heat 18–20°C, germination may take several weeks
Athyrium filix-femina	Sow spores on to sterilized compost, cover with clear polythene film straight after sowing. Require light but not direct sunlight, cool conditions. Germination takes several weeks
Athyrium niponicum	Sow spores on to sterilized compost, cover with clear polythene film straight after sowing. Require light but not direct sunlight, cool conditions. Germination takes several weeks
Aubrieta × *hybrida* cultivars	Can be sown in cold frame or outdoor bed. Quicker germination with bottom heat
Aucuba japonica	Can be sown in cold frame or outdoor bed. Quicker germination with bottom heat
Baptisia australis	Nick seed or rub with sandpaper and sow fresh in autumn
Begonia × *benariensis* cultivars	Sow on surface, quicker germination with bottom heat
Begonia × *semperflorens* cultivars	Sow on surface, quicker germination with bottom heat
Bellis perennis cultivars	Can be sown in cold frame or outdoor bed. Quicker germination with bottom heat

(continued overleaf)

continued

Plant	Propagation Requirements
Berberis darwinii	Cold period (4°C) for 18–20 weeks
Berberis thunbergia	Cold period (4°C) for 8–10 weeks
Berberis verruculosa	Cold period (4°C) for 8–10 weeks
Berberis wilsoniae	Cold period (4°C) for 8–10 weeks
Betula nigra	4 weeks cold period (4°C) and sow seed on surface; do not cover
Betula pendula	4 weeks cold period (4°C) and sow seed on surface; do not cover
Borago officinalis	Can be sown in cold frame or outdoor bed
Briza media	Can be sown in cold frame or outdoor bed; germination can be erratic
Brunnera macrophylla	Can be sown in cold frame or outdoor bed
Buddleja alternifolia	Can be sown in cold frame or outdoor bed
Buddleja davidii	Can be sown in cold frame or outdoor bed
Calamintha nepeta	Bottom heat 18–20°C, germination can be erratic
Calendula officinalis	Can be sown in cold frame or outdoor bed
Calla palustris	Can be sown in cold frame or outdoor bed
Camellia japonica	Sow seed when ripe, if stored do not allow to dry out
Camellia sasanqua	Sow seed when ripe, if stored do not allow to dry out
Campanula carpatica	Sow on surface, can be sown in cold frame or outdoor bed. Quicker germination with bottom heat
Campanula lactiflora	Sow on surface, can be sown in cold frame or outdoor bed. Quicker germination with bottom heat
Campanula persicifolia	Sow on surface, can be sown in cold frame or outdoor bed. Quicker germination with bottom heat
Campanula portenschlagiana	Sow on surface, can be sown in cold frame or outdoor bed. Quicker germination with bottom heat
Campsis radicans	2–4 weeks cold period (4°C), then bottom heat of 18–20°C
Carpinus betulus	20–24 weeks cold period (4°C)
Catalpa bignonioides	Soak seed for 24 hours in warm water prior to sowing. Germination is quicker with bottom heat
Cedrus atlantica Glauca Group	Soak seed for 24 hours, then cold period for 6–8 weeks (4°C), then bottom heat 15–18°C. Germination can be erratic
Cedrus deodara	Soak seed for 24 hours, then cold period for 2–4 weeks (4°C), then bottom heat 15–18°C. Germination can be erratic
Celosia argentea	Bottom heat 20–22°C
Centaurea nigra	Bottom heat 15–20°C
Centranthus ruber	Bottom heat 18–20°C
Cephalaria gigante	Bottom heat 18–20°C
Cercidiphyllum japonicum	Can be sown in cold frame or outdoor bed, spring germination quicker with bottom heat
Cercis siliquastrum	Soak in hot water for 24 hours, then cold period for 1–2 weeks (4°C), sow at 15–18°C
Chamaecyparis lawsoniana	Soak seed for 24 hours in warm water, then 4 weeks cold period (4°C)
Cheilanthes lanosa	Sow spores on to sterilized compost, cover with clear polythene film straight after sowing. Require light but not direct sunlight, cool conditions. Germination takes several weeks
Choisya ternata	Can be sown in cold frame or outdoor bed
Cirsium rivulare	Can be sown in cold frame or outdoor bed. Quicker germination with bottom heat
Clematis vitalba	Bottom heat 18–20°C, germination very slow, can be up to a year and erratic

(continued overleaf)

continued

Plant	Propagation Requirements
Cleome hassleriana cultivars	Sow on surface, quicker germination with bottom heat
Coleus × blumei cultivars	Sow on surface, quicker germination with bottom heat
Cordyline australis	Require bottom heat 18–22°C, germination erratic and can take several weeks
Coreopsis grandiflora and cultivars	Bottom heat 20–24°C
Coreopsis verticillate	Bottom heat 20–24°C
Cornus alba	Keep seeds moist during 12–14 weeks cold period (4°C) prior to sowing
Cornus canadensis	Keep seeds moist during 16–20 weeks cold period (4°C) prior to sowing
Cornus controversa	Keep seeds moist during warm period of 16 weeks at 20°C followed by 8–10 weeks cold period (4°C) prior to sowing
Cornus kousa	Keep seeds moist during warm period of 2–4 weeks at 20°C followed by 12–16 weeks cold period (4°C) prior to sowing
Cornus sanguinea	Keep seeds moist during 12–14 weeks cold period (4°C) prior to sowing
Corylus avellana	Require cold period of 6 weeks (4°C)
Cosmos bipinnatus and cultivars	Bottom heat 18–20°C
Cotoneaster conspicuous	Soak seed prior to 12–16 weeks cold period (4°C)
Cotoneaster franchetii	Soak seed prior to 12–16 weeks cold period (4°C)
Cotoneaster microphyllus	Soak seed prior to 12–16 weeks cold period (4°C)
Cotoneaster simonaii	Soak seed prior to 12–16 weeks cold period (4°C)
Crambe cordifolia	Require bottom heat 18–20°C, germinates erratically over several weeks
Crambe maritima	Require bottom heat 18–20°C, germinates erratically over several weeks
Crataegus laevigata	8–12 weeks warm period 15–18°C followed by 28–40 weeks cold period (4°C)
Crataegus monogyna	8–12 weeks warm period 15–18°C followed by 24–32 weeks cold period (4°C)
Cuphea hyssopifolia cultivars	Sow on surface, quicker germination with bottom heat
Cuphea ignea cultivars	Sow on surface, quicker germination with bottom heat
Cyclamen coum	Soak seeds in water for 12–24 hours, bottom heat 15°C, seeds must be in complete darkness, germination erratic over several weeks
Cyclamen hederifolium	Soak seeds in water for 12–24 hours, bottom heat 15°C, seeds must be in complete darkness, germination erratic over several weeks
Cyclamen persicum	Soak seeds in water for 12–24 hours, bottom heat 15°C, seeds must be in complete darkness, germination erratic over several weeks
Cynara cardunculus	Can be sown in cold frame or outdoor bed. Quicker germination with bottom heat
Delphinium elatum cultivars	Can be sown in cold frame or outdoor bed. Quicker germination with bottom heat
Delphinium grandiflorum cultivars	Can be sown in cold frame or outdoor bed. Quicker germination with bottom heat
Deschampsia cespitosa	Require bottom heat 18–20°C, germination can be erratic over several weeks
Dianthus barbatus cultivars	Can be sown in cold frame or outdoor bed. Quicker germination with bottom heat
Dianthus chinensis cultivars	Require bottom heat 18–20°C
Dicentra spectabilis	Can be sown in cold frame or outdoor bed. Quicker germination with bottom heat, germination can take several weeks and is very erratic
Dichondra argentea	Bottom heat 20–24°C
Digitalis × mertonensis	Bottom heat 15–20°C
Digitalis parviflora	Bottom heat 15–20°C

(continued overleaf)

continued

Plant	Propagation Requirements
Digitalis purpurea and cultivars	Bottom heat 15–20°C
Doronicum orientale cultivars	Sow seed on surface, bottom heat 18–20°C
Dryopteris affinis	Sow spores on to sterilized compost, cover with clear polythene film straight after sowing. Require light but not direct sunlight, cool conditions. Germination takes several weeks
Dryopteris cycadina	Sow spores on to sterilized compost, cover with clear polythene film straight after sowing. Require light but not direct sunlight, cool conditions. Germination takes several weeks
Dryopteris erythrosora	Sow spores on to sterilized compost, cover with clear polythene film straight after sowing. Require light but not direct sunlight, cool conditions. Germination takes several weeks
Dryopteris filix–mas	Sow spores on to sterilized compost, cover with clear polythene film straight after sowing. Require light but not direct sunlight, cool conditions. Germination takes several weeks
Dryopteris wallichiana	Sow spores on to sterilized compost, cover with clear polythene film straight after sowing. Require light but not direct sunlight, cool conditions. Germination takes several weeks
Echinacea purpurea	Sow seed on surface, bottom heat 22–24°C
Echinops bannaticus	Bottom heat 18–20°C
Echinops ritro	Bottom heat 18–20°C
Erigeron karvinskianus	Sow on surface, quicker germination with bottom heat
Eryngium planum	2–3 weeks cold period (4°C)
Eryngium variifolium	2–3 weeks cold period (4°C)
Erysimum cheiri and cultivars	Can be sown in cold frame or outdoor bed. Quicker germination with bottom heat
Eucalyptus gunnii	Bottom heat 18–22°C
Euonymus alatus	12 weeks warm period, seed must be kept moist, followed by 12 weeks cold period (4°C)
Euonymus europaeus	12 weeks warm period, seed must be kept moist, followed by 12–14 weeks cold period (4°C)
Euphorbia shillingii	Can be sown in cold frame or outdoor bed. Quicker germination with bottom heat
Fagus sylvatica	16 weeks cold period (4°C)
Fallopia baldschuanica	Can be sown in cold frame or outdoor bed. Quicker germination with bottom heat
Fatsia japonica	Sow seed on surface, bottom heat 18–20°C, germination erratic
Filipendula rubra	Can be sown in cold frame or outdoor bed. Quicker germination with bottom heat
Filipendula ulmaria	Can be sown in cold frame or outdoor bed. Quicker germination with bottom heat
Foeniculum vulgare cultivars	Can be sown in cold frame or outdoor bed. Quicker germination with bottom heat
Gazania cultivars	Germinate quicker with bottom heat
Genista hispanica	8–12 weeks cold period (4°C)
Geranium cinereum	Can be sown in cold frame or outdoor bed. Quicker germination with bottom heat
Geranium clarkei	Can be sown in cold frame or outdoor bed. Quicker germination with bottom heat
Geranium macrorrhizum	Can be sown in cold frame or outdoor bed. Quicker germination with bottom heat
Geranium nodosum	Can be sown in cold frame or outdoor bed. Quicker germination with bottom heat
Geranium phaeum	Can be sown in cold frame or outdoor bed. Quicker germination with bottom heat
Geranium psilostemon	Can be sown in cold frame or outdoor bed. Quicker germination with bottom heat
Geranium sanguineum	Can be sown in cold frame or outdoor bed. Quicker germination with bottom heat
Geum 'Borisii'	Germinate quicker with bottom heat
Gleditsia triacanthos	Soak seeds for 24 hours prior to sowing
Gunnera manicata	Surface sow with bottom heat 20–24°C, keep moist at all times, germination erratic
Helianthus annuus and cultivars	Can be sown in cold frame or outdoor bed. Quicker germination with bottom heat

(continued overleaf)

continued

Plant	Propagation Requirements
Helleborus foetidus	Sow as soon as seed is ripe, germination erratic
Helleborus × orientalis cultivars	Sow as soon as seed is ripe, germination erratic
Hippophae rhamnoides	12–14 weeks cold period (4°C)
Humulus lupulus	Soak seed for 12–24 hours prior to sowing, keep seed moist at all times, no heat required, germination takes 4–6 weeks
Hypericum androsaemum	Can be sown in cold frame or outdoor bed, germination very slow and erratic
Hyssopus officinalis	Can be sown in cold frame or outdoor bed. Quicker germination with bottom heat
Iberis sempervirens 'Snowflake'	Sow seed on surface, can be sown in cold frame or outdoor bed. Quicker germination with bottom heat
Ilex aquifolium	40 weeks warm period at 15°C followed by 24 weeks cold period (4°C), germination slow and erratic
Impatiens walleriana cultivars	Surface sow, bottom heat 20–22°C, germination can be erratic
Impatiens 'New Guinea' cultivars	Surface sow, bottom heat 20–22°C, germination can be erratic
Iris foetidissima	Soak seed in warm water for 24 hours then cold period for 12–14 weeks (4°C), germination erratic
Iris sibirica	Soak seed in warm water for 24 hours then cold period for 12–14 weeks (4°C), germination erratic
Jasminum nudiflorum	Can be sown in cold frame or outdoor bed. Quicker germination with bottom heat
Juglans nigra	16 weeks cold period (4°C)
Juniperus communis	12–52 weeks warm period at 18–20°C, followed by 20–24 weeks cold period at 4°C. Germination erratic
Kalmia latifolia	8 weeks cold period (4°C) then surface sow with bottom heat 18–20°C
Kerria japonica	14–16 weeks cold period (4°C)
Knautia macedonica	4 weeks cold period (4°C) then surface sow, no heat required, germination erratic
Koeleria glauca	Surface sow with bottom heat 18–20°C
Koelreuteria paniculata	Scarify seed with sandpaper or similar, followed by cold period of 12–14 weeks (4°C). Germination quicker with bottom heat
Lantana camara	Sow with bottom heat 18–21°C
Lathyrus odorata cultivars	Soak seeds overnight in warm water or scarify with sandpaper or similar. Sow at 16–20°C
Laurentia axillaris cultivars	Surface sow, bottom heat of 18–20°C
Laurus nobilis	8–12 weeks cold period (4°C)
Leon topodium alpinum	Surface sow, quicker germination with bottom heat
Levisticum officinale	Can be sown in cold frame or outdoor bed. Quicker germination with bottom heat
Lewisia hybrids	5–6 weeks cold period (4°C), do not require bottom heat, germination erratic
Liatris spicata	Can be sown in cold frame or outdoor bed. Quicker germination with bottom heat
Ligustrum delavayanum	8–12 weeks cold period
Ligustrum lucidum	8–12 weeks cold period
Ligustrum ovalifolium	8–12 weeks cold period
Ligustrum vulgare	8–12 weeks cold period
Limonium platyphyllum	Germinate quicker with bottom heat

(continued overleaf)

continued

Plant	Propagation Requirements
Liquidambar styraciflua	Keep seeds moist during 4–12 weeks cold period (4°C). Germination quicker with bottom heat
Liriodendron tulipifera	Keep seeds moist during 4–12 weeks cold period (4°C). Germination quicker with bottom heat
Lobelia erinus cultivars	Bottom heat 20–24°C, germination erratic over 2–4 weeks
Lupinus cultivars	Soak seed for 2–3 days, bottom heat 18–20°C, germination erratic over several weeks
Luzula sylvatica	Bottom heat 18–20°C
Lychnis chalcedonica	Surface sow, can be sown in cold frame or outdoor bed. Quicker germination with bottom heat
Lychnis flos-cuculi	Surface sow, can be sown in cold frame or outdoor bed. Quicker germination with bottom heat
Lysimachia clethroides	Surface sow, bottom heat 16–18°C, germination slow and erratic
Lythrum salicaria	Surface sow, can be sown in cold frame or outdoor bed. Quicker germination with bottom heat, keep moist
Magnolia grandiflora	Clean pulp from seed thoroughly, sow immediately or cold period of 10–14 weeks (4°C)
Magnolia kobus	Soak seed for 24–48 hours, cold period 24–28 weeks (4°C)
Mahonia aquifolium	Remove all pulp from seed; cold period 16–18 weeks (4°C)
Malus sylvestris	Soak seed for 24 hours, warm period at 18–20°C for 2–3 weeks followed by cold period of 12–14 weeks (4°C)
Malus tschonoskii	12–14 weeks cold period (4°C), germination slow and erratic
Mandevilla splendens	Bottom heat 20–24°C
Matteuccia struthiopteris	Sow spores on to sterilized compost, cover with clear polythene film straight after sowing. Require light but not direct sunlight, cool conditions. Germination takes several weeks
Melica altissima 'Atropurpurea'	Can be sown in cold frame or outdoor bed. Quicker germination with bottom heat
Mentha spicata	Can be sown in cold frame or outdoor bed. Quicker germination with bottom heat
Mespilus germanica	No bottom heat, germination slow and erratic
Metasequoia glyptostroboides	6 weeks cold period (4°C) followed by bottom heat 18–20°C
Milium effusum 'Aureum'	Can be sown in cold frame or outdoor bed. Quicker germination with bottom heat
Monarda cultivars	Can be sown in cold frame or outdoor bed. Quicker germination with bottom heat
Mukdenia rossii	Can be sown in cold frame or outdoor bed. Quicker germination with bottom heat
Myosotis sylvatica	Can be sown in cold frame or outdoor bed. Quicker germination with bottom heat
Myrtus communis	Soak seed for 24 hours then bottom heat 10–24°C
Nemesia cultivars	Bottom heat 15–18°C
Nicotiana alata cultivars	Surface sow, bottom heat 18–20°C
Nicotiana sylvestris	Surface sow, bottom heat 18–20°C
Ocimum basilicum	Germinates quicker with bottom heat
Olea europaea	Soak seed for 3–4 days followed by bottom heat 18–20°C. Germination slow and erratic
Origanum vulgare	Can be sown in cold frame or outdoor bed. Quicker germination with bottom heat
Osmunda regalis	Sow spores on to sterilized compost, cover with clear polythene film straight after sowing. Require light but not direct sunlight, cool conditions. Germination takes several weeks
Osteospermum cultivars	Bottom heat 16–18°C
Papaver nudicaule and cultivars	Can be sown in cold frame or outdoor bed
Papaver orientale and cultivars	Can be sown in cold frame or outdoor bed. Quicker germination with bottom heat

(continued overleaf)

continued

Plant	Propagation Requirements
Parthenocissus henryana	10–12 weeks cold period (4°C)
Parthenocissus quinquefolia	10–12 weeks cold period (4°C)
Parthenocissus tricuspidata	10–12 weeks cold period (4°C)
Paulownia tomentosa	Surface sow, bottom heat 18–20°C, germination over several weeks
Pelargonium × peltatum cultivars	Bottom heat 21–24°C
Pelargonium × zonale cultivars	Bottom heat 21–24°C
Pennisetum alopecuroides	Surface sow, germinates quicker with bottom heat
Pennisetum glaucum	Surface sow, germinates quicker with bottom heat
Pennisetum orientale	Surface sow, germinates quicker with bottom heat
Pennisetum villosum	Surface sow, germinates quicker with bottom heat
Penstemon	Bottom heat 18–20°C, germination erratic
Persicaria amplexicaulis	Germinates quicker with bottom heat
Petunia × atkinsiana cultivars	Bottom heat 18–20°C
Petunia × grandiflora cultivars	Bottom heat 18–20°C
Petunia × grandiflora	Bottom heat 18–20°C
Phlomis fruticosa	Can be sown in cold frame or outdoor bed
Phlomis italica	Can be sown in cold frame or outdoor bed
Phlomis russeliana	Can be sown in cold frame or outdoor bed
Phoenix canariensis	Soak seed for 48 hours, bottom heat 22–25°C
Phormium tenax	Bottom heat 18–20°C, germination slow and erratic
Physostegia virginiana	Surface sow, bottom heat 18–20°C
Picea abies	Soak seed for 24 hours followed by 6–8 weeks cold period (4°C)
Picea glauca	Soak seed for 24 hours followed by 6–8 weeks cold period (4°C)
Picea omorika	Soak seed for 24 hours followed by 6–8 weeks cold period (4°C)
Pinus nigra	Can be sown in cold frame or outdoor bed
Pinus sylvestris	Can be sown in cold frame or outdoor bed
Pittosporum tenuifolium	Soak in hot water for a few minutes, then sow in cold frame or outdoor bed
Pittosporum tobira	Soak in hot water for a few minutes, then sow in cold frame or outdoor bed
Polemonium caeruleum	Bottom heat 15–18°C
Polypodium vulgare	Sow spores on to sterilized compost, cover with clear polythene film straight after sowing. Require light but not direct sunlight, cool conditions. Germination takes several weeks
Polystichum aculeatum	Sow spores on to sterilized compost, cover with clear polythene film straight after sowing. Require light but not direct sunlight, cool conditions. Germination takes several weeks
Polystichum munitum	Sow spores on to sterilized compost, cover with clear polythene film straight after sowing. Require light but not direct sunlight, cool conditions. Germination takes several weeks
Polystichum polyblepharum	Sow spores on to sterilized compost, cover with clear polythene film straight after sowing. Require light but not direct sunlight, cool conditions. Germination takes several weeks
Polystichum setiferum	Sow spores on to sterilized compost, cover with clear polythene film straight after sowing. Require light but not direct sunlight, cool conditions. Germination takes several weeks
Polystichum tsus-simense	Sow spores on to sterilized compost, cover with clear polythene film straight after sowing. Require light but not direct sunlight, cool conditions. Germination takes several weeks
Populus alba	Sow as soon as seed is ripe in spring

(continued overleaf)

continued

Plant	Propagation Requirements
Populus tremula	Sow as soon as seed is ripe in spring
Primula veris	Can be sown in cold frame or outdoor bed. Quicker germination with bottom heat, germination can be erratic
Primula vialii	Can be sown in cold frame or outdoor bed. Quicker germination with bottom heat, germination can be erratic
Primula vulgaris	Can be sown in cold frame or outdoor bed. Quicker germination with bottom heat, germination can be erratic
Prunus avium	8–10 weeks cold period
Prunus laurocerasus	8–10 weeks cold period
Prunus lusitanica	8–10 weeks cold period
Prunus padus	18–20 weeks cold period
Prunus sargentii	8–10 weeks cold period
Prunus serrula	8–10 weeks cold period
Prunus spinosa	8–10 weeks cold period
Pulsatilla vulgaris	Can be sown in cold frame or outdoor bed. Quicker germination with bottom heat
Quercus cerris	Sow outdoors as soon as seed as ripe
Quercus ilex	Sow outdoors as soon as seed as ripe
Quercus robur	Sow outdoors as soon as seed as ripe
Quercus rubra	Sow outdoors as soon as seed as ripe
Rhamnus cathartica	Keep seed moist for cold period of 8–10 weeks (4°C), then sow outside
Rheum palmatum var. tanguticum	Soak seed for 24 hours prior to sowing
Rhodochiton atrosanguineum	Bottom heat 16–18°C, germination can be erratic
Rhododendron ponticum	Surface sow when ripe in outdoor bed
Rosa canina	Warm period 18–20°C for 8 weeks, then cold period (4°C) for 12–16 weeks. Keep seed moist throughout
Rosa rugosa	18–36 weeks cold period (4°C)
Rosmarinus officinalis	Surface sow, can be sown in cold frame or outdoor bed. Quicker germination with bottom heat, germination can be erratic
Ruscus aculeatus	8–12 warm period 15°C followed by 12–16 weeks cold period (4°C)
Salvia farinacea	Surface sow, bottom heat 18–22°C
Salvia officinalis	Surface sow, bottom heat 15–18°C
Salvia splendens cultivars	Surface sow, bottom heat 18–22°C
Sanguisorba canadensis	Can be sown in cold frame or outdoor bed. Quicker germination with bottom heat
Sanguisorba officinalis	Can be sown in cold frame or outdoor bed. Quicker germination with bottom heat
Sanvitalia procumbens cultivars	Bottom heat 18–20°C
Scabiosa caucasica cultivars	Bottom heat 18–20°C
Sequoiadendron giganteum	Cold period (4°C) for 10–12 weeks
Sidalcea cultivars	Cold period (4°C) for 4 weeks, then bottom heat 15°C
Silene dioica	Can be sown in cold frame or outdoor bed. Quicker germination with bottom heat
Sisyrinchium striatum	Can be sown in cold frame or outdoor bed, germination can be erratic
Sorbus aucuparia	2 weeks warm period 15°C followed by 28–30 weeks cold period (4°C)

(continued overleaf)

continued

Plant	Propagation Requirements
Sporobolus heterolepis	Can be sown in cold frame or outdoor bed. Quicker germination with bottom heat
Stevia rebaudiana	Bottom heat 25–28°C
Stipa gigantea	Can be sown in cold frame or outdoor bed. Quicker germination with bottom heat
Stipa tenuissima	Can be sown in cold frame or outdoor bed. Quicker germination with bottom heat
Succisa pratensis	Can be sown in cold frame or outdoor bed
Tagetes × erecta cultivars	Bottom heat 20–24°C
Tagetes × patula cultivars	Surface sow, bottom heat 20–24°C
Tamarix tetandra	Can be sown in cold frame or outdoor bed. Quicker germination with bottom heat
Tellima grandiflora	Can be sown in cold frame or outdoor bed. Quicker germination with bottom heat, germination can be erratic
Thalictrum delavayi	Can be sown in cold frame or outdoor bed. Quicker germination with bottom heat
Thunbergia alata cultivars	Bottom heat 18–20°C
Thymus vulgaris	Can be sown in cold frame or outdoor bed. Quicker germination with bottom heat
Tilia cordata	16 weeks warm period 15°C followed by 16 weeks cold period (4°C), keep seed moist throughout
Tulbaghia violacea	Can be sown in cold frame or outdoor bed. Quicker germination with bottom heat
Uncinia rubra	Can be sown in cold frame or outdoor bed. Quicker germination with bottom heat
Verbascum chaixii	Can be sown in cold frame or outdoor bed. Quicker germination with bottom heat
Verbascum cultivars	Can be sown in cold frame or outdoor bed. Quicker germination with bottom heat
Verbena bonariensis	Can be sown in cold frame or outdoor bed. Quicker germination with bottom heat
Verbena ridiga	Can be sown in cold frame or outdoor bed. Quicker germination with bottom heat
Viburnum lantana	Soak seed for 24 hours followed by cold period 10–12 weeks (4°C)
Viburnum opulus	6–8 weeks warm period 15°C followed by 8–12 weeks cold period (4°C), germination erratic
Viola cornuta and cultivars	Can be sown in cold frame or outdoor bed. Quicker germination with bottom heat
Viola × wittrockiana cultivars	Can be sown in cold frame or outdoor bed. Quicker germination with bottom heat
Watsonia pillansii	Bottom heat 16–20°C, germination can be slow
Wisteria floribunda	Can be sown in cold frame or outdoor bed. Quicker germination with bottom heat
Wisteria sinensis	Can be sown in cold frame or outdoor bed. Quicker germination with bottom heat
Zinnia elegans cultivars	Can be sown in cold frame or outdoor bed. Quicker germination with bottom heat

CHAPTER 4

SOFTWOOD CUTTINGS

What are Softwood Cuttings?

Softwood cuttings are taken between late spring and early summer from the current season's growth on the plant. A wide variety of plants can be propagated from softwood cuttings, ranging from trees to shrubs, herbaceous perennials, alpines and houseplants. Herbaceous perennials are often propagated from basal softwood cuttings, which are young shoots taken from the crown of the plant.

The material is all juvenile, soft and succulent growth, with high levels of hormones naturally occurring to promote rooting. The time period that softwood material is available varies from species to species, but between two and eight weeks after growth starts is the average time span that softwood material is available. The material used should be healthy, but not spindly or weak, and side shoots or lateral shoots are generally preferable, although stem-tip cuttings can be used for some plants. Plants propagated by this method usually require a protected environment, and to propagate commercially, bottom heat is needed for most woody subjects, although many herbaceous plants and sub-shrubs will root without bottom heat.

Salvia officinalis 'Purpurea'.

Softwood cuttings root quite quickly in the right environment, taking between two and five weeks, but the material needs to be collected early in the day, when it is cool, and the material needs to be kept moist and cool until it is prepared. White polythene bags that have been lightly dampened with water inside, helps to keep the material turgid. The material may only take a few minutes to dry out, and this will severely affect its rooting ability. Only collect enough cutting material that can be dealt with before it dries out or, alternatively, most softwood material can be cold-stored for a day or two at round 4°C.

Softwood cuttings are usually quite small in comparison to hardwood or semi-ripe cuttings. Cutting size depends on species but ranges from 7.5 to 12.5 cm (3–5 in) long. Any flower bud should be removed along with the lower leaves.

Cuttings should have at least two nodes, with the basal cut taken just below a node, and the top cut just above a node, if more than one section of a stem is being used. For plants that have large leaves, the remaining leaves can be cut back to reduce transpiration, and to help prevent diseases, such as botrytis, from the leaves touching each other. Cutting back the leaves also reduces the amount of space these large-leaved species take up on a propagation bench, but does leave the cuttings more prone to disease, so a preventative fungicide application may be used. The use of rooting hormone will depend on the species, as softwood cuttings may not require the rooting hormone, due to the high quantities already in the cutting at that time of year.

Most softwood cuttings are nodal, but some plants will root well from internodal cuttings. For plants that have long internodes this can be advantageous and make the cuttings more manageable, e.g. *Fuchsia* cultivars. As with all stem cuttings, several cuttings may be taken from one stem or shoot, as long as the material is suitable.

Basal softwood cuttings are taken mainly from herbaceous perennials. Herbaceous perennials are plants that die down, usually in the winter, and produce new growth from the crown of the plant each year. This new growth is often vigorous and ideal for basal softwood cuttings, including species such as *Delphinium*, *Lupinus*, *Salvia*, *Phlox* and *Aster* species. The cutting material is taken when new growth has started, and the new growth should be about 6–10 cm $\left(2\frac{1}{2}-4\text{ in}\right)$ long. Use a sharp knife and cut as close to the base as possible, where the crown of the plant may be slightly woody. Basal cuttings can root very easily and may sometimes already have a small amount of root at the bottom where they were separated from the parent plant.

Equipment

- Secateurs, snips or knife.
- Cell trays.
- Good-quality cutting compost, moist and free-draining.
- Rooting hormone for difficult-to-root subjects.
- Heated benches or propagators required for most woody plants, especially on a large scale.
- Mist system – open or closed depending on species – to maintain humidity.
- Shading.
- Labels/pens.

Advantages and disadvantages of softwood cuttings

Softwood Cuttings Advantages	Softwood Cuttings Disadvantages
Juvenile material, usually easy to root	Material needs to be used quickly after collection
Quicker to root than other types of cutting	Usually requires a protected environment – more expensive
Large quantities can be produced	Need careful management
Suitable for a wide range of plants	

Taking Softwood Cuttings

Step 1: Select material.

Step 3: Remove the bottom leaves of plants with larger leaves to aid insertion. Insert into rooting hormone, if necessary.

Step 2: Make the cutting by cutting the stem just below a node at the base and just above a node at the tip, ensuring a minimum of two nodes.

Step 4: Insert cuttings into a prepared cell tray. Place in a protected environment.

Fuchsia small-leaf cuttings.

Basal softwood cuttings follow the same steps, but are generally used on herbaceous perennials. The propagation material is selected from young shoots at the base or crown of the parent plant, and then prepared as for softwood cuttings.

Sedum purpurea.

Taking Softwood Cuttings – Large-Leaved

Step 1: Select material.

Step 2: Make the cutting by cutting just below a node at the base and just above a node at the tip, ensuring a minimum of two nodes.

Step 3: Remove the bottom leaves of plants with larger leaves to aid insertion.

Step 5: Insert cuttings into a prepared cell tray. Place in a protected environment.

Materials and Environments

Softwood cuttings may require bottom heat, humidity, shading, or diffuse light levels depending on the plant. Adequate moisture (but not too wet), well-drained soil or compost and good aeration are also beneficial. Glasshouses or polytunnels are suitable, and heated propagators can be used in the domestic environment. Softwood cuttings that do not require bottom heat – many herbaceous plants and sub-shrubs, e.g. *Rosmarinus*, *Salvia*, *Achillea* and *Sedum*, will usually still need a protected environment, such as low polythene tunnels and shading.

Glasshouse or Polytunnel and Bottom Heat

Cuttings can be inserted directly into cell trays, or beds filled with good-quality cutting compost and placed on bottom heat in glasshouses or polytunnels. Bottom heat of 18–23°C is generally successful, but individual species differ. Air temperatures up to 30–32°C inside a mist or fog system are acceptable, but higher than this may be detrimental to rooting. An open mist system

Step 4: Cut the leaves on large-leaved species to aid insertion. Insert into rooting hormone, if necessary.

can be used, or closed mist where the mist system is enclosed under polythene keeps humidity levels higher.

Low Polythene without Bottom Heat

Low tunnels can be created over glasshouse benches, inside polytunnels or even outdoors in a sheltered situation. Hoops can be placed over the propagation site and covered with polythene and shade netting, if necessary. Mist can be used to maintain humidity and reduce transpiration.

Aftercare and Potting On

Softwood cuttings should be checked regularly and failed propagules removed to reduce the risk of disease. Good hygiene is essential in protected environments and can significantly reduce the need for fungicide applications, as botrytis can spread quickly to healthy cuttings if left unchecked. Temperature and humidity fluctuations should also be monitored, where possible, to ensure stability; and check if shading should be added or removed, as required.

After good root development has taken place, the cuttings can be be weaned from the protected environment they were in over a period of time, gradually reducing heat and humidity over one to three weeks. This can be achieved by lowering the bottom heat temperature, reducing frequency of misting and opening plastic covers for periods if propagules were covered. Shading is still important, as softwood cuttings can become stressed under high light levels.

Pot on into the appropriate next size container, using a good-quality compost, with a higher fertilizer ratio than the rooting medium.

Potting on into the next stage should be done as soon as there is sufficient root, as the earlier potting can increase the quality and survival rate of the propagule over winter.

Failures in the rooted cuttings can occur over the following winter, so protected environments may still be required, either cold tunnels or cold glass, or heated frost protection. Fleece over low tunnels on benches can provide 3–4°C increase on ambient temperature. Even though the plants may be very hardy once mature, at the rooted cutting and liner stage they are susceptible to frost and other environmental stresses. Overwatering is a common cause of failure when over-wintering softwood cuttings, particularly on deciduous and herbaceous subjects, so managing the root environment, ensuring that is does not become too wet, is crucial.

Plants to Propagate from Softwood Cuttings

The difficulty is subjective and may vary according to locality and availability of material. A wide variety of plants may be propagated by more than one method, so whilst softwood cuttings may be an option, some may be more successful as semi-ripe or hardwood. The conditions suggested do not mean that rooting will not take place without those conditions, just that it may be slower or a lower percentage take.

Rooting hormone should be applied according to manufacturers' recommendations.

Key to difficulty rating

Easy	Roots easily, high-percentage rooting, requires little or no protected environments
Medium	May require some hormone-rooting treatment, reasonable rooting percentage, rooting speed and percentage improved with protected environment
Difficult	Difficult to root, low rooting percentage, requires high level of protected environment

Plants to propagate from softwood cuttings and their difficulty rating

Plant	Propagation Requirements
Abelia 'Edward Goucher'	Bottom heat and mist
Abelia grandiflora	Bottom heat and mist
Abelia grandiflora 'Francis Mason'	Bottom heat and mist
Abelia grandiflora 'Gold Spot'	Bottom heat and mist
Abelia schumanii	Bottom heat and mist
Abeliophyllum distichum	Bottom heat and mist
Abutilon cultivars	Low tunnel
Acer campestre cultivars	Mist and bottom heat
Acer griseum cultivars	Mist and bottom heat
Acer palmatum cultivars	Mist and bottom heat
Actinidia kolomikta	Bottom heat and tunnel
Alnus glutinosa	Bottom heat and tunnel
Alnus incana	Bottom heat and tunnel
Amelanchier canadensis cultivars	Bottom heat and mist
Amelanchier lamarckii cultivars	Bottom heat and mist
Anaphalis triplinervis cultivars	Basal cuttings, low tunnel, quicker with bottom heat
Angelonia angustifolia cultivars	Bottom heat and tunnel or glasshouse
Arabis caucasica cultivars	Stem-tip cuttings, quicker with bottom heat, tunnel or glass
Argyranthemum frutescens cultivars	Basal cuttings, quicker with bottom heat, tunnel or glass
Artemisia aborescens	Basal cuttings, quicker with bottom heat, tunnel or glass
Aster × frikartii cultivars	Basal cuttings, quicker with bottom heat, tunnel or glass
Begonia boliviensis cultivars	Basal cuttings, quicker with bottom heat, tunnel or glass
Betula nigra cultivars	Mist and bottom heat
Betula pendula cultivars	Mist and bottom heat
Betula utilis var. *jacquemontii*	Mist and bottom heat
Bidens ferulifolia cultivars	Bottom heat and tunnel or glasshouse
Brachyscome × multifida cultivars	Bottom heat and tunnel or glasshouse
Buddleja alternifolia	Quicker with bottom heat, tunnel or glass
Buddleja davidii cultivars	Quicker with bottom heat, tunnel or glass
Buxus microphylla	Quicker with bottom heat, tunnel or glass
Buxus sempervirens cultivars	Quicker with bottom heat, tunnel or glass
Calibrachoa cultivars	Bottom heat and tunnel or glasshouse
Callicarpa bodinieri 'Profusion'	Quicker with bottom heat, tunnel or glass
Campanula glomerata cultivars	Basal cuttings, quicker with bottom heat, tunnel or glass
Campanula lactiflora cultivars	Basal cuttings, quicker with bottom heat, tunnel or glass
Campanula persicifolia cultivars	Basal cuttings, quicker with bottom heat, tunnel or glass
Campsis radicans	Quicker with bottom heat, tunnel or glass
Campsis × tagliabuana 'Madame Galen'	Quicker with bottom heat, tunnel or glass
Carpinus betulus cultivars	Quicker with bottom heat, tunnel or glass
Caryopteris × clandonensis cultivars	Quicker with bottom heat, tunnel or glass

(continued overleaf)

continued

Plant	Propagation Requirements
Ceanothus arboreus 'Trewithen Blue'	Bottom heat and mist
Ceanothus 'Autumnal Blue'	Bottom heat and mist
Ceanothus 'Blue Cushion'	Bottom heat and mist
Ceanothus 'Blue Mound'	Bottom heat and mist
Ceanothus 'Concha'	Bottom heat and mist
Ceanothus 'Italian Skies'	Bottom heat and mist
Ceanothus 'Puget Blue'	Bottom heat and mist
Ceanothus thyrsiflorus var. *repens*	Bottom heat and mist
Ceratostigma plumbaginoides	Quicker with bottom heat, tunnel or glass
Ceratostigma willmottianum	Quicker with bottom heat, tunnel or glass
Chaenomeles × *superba* cultivars	Quicker with bottom heat, tunnel or glass
Cistus 'Grayswood Pink'	Quicker with bottom heat, tunnel or glass
Cistus pulverentus	Quicker with bottom heat, tunnel or glass
Cistus purpureus	Quicker with bottom heat, tunnel or glass
Cistus 'Silver Pink'	Quicker with bottom heat, tunnel or glass
Cistus × *dansereaui* 'Decumbens'	Quicker with bottom heat, tunnel or glass
Cistus × *hybridus*	Quicker with bottom heat, tunnel or glass
Cistus × *pulverulentus* 'Sunset'	Quicker with bottom heat, tunnel or glass
Cistus × *purpureus*	Quicker with bottom heat, tunnel or glass
Clematis large-flowered hybrids	Bottom heat and mist
Clematis integrifolia cultivars	Bottom heat and mist
Clematis montana cultivars	Bottom heat and mist
Clematis viticella cultivars	Bottom heat and mist
Coleus × *blumei* cultivars	Quicker with bottom heat, tunnel or glass
Coreopsis verticillata cultivars	Basal cuttings, quicker with bottom heat, tunnel or glass
Cornus alba cultivars	Quicker with bottom heat, tunnel or glass
Cornus sanguine cultivars	Quicker with bottom heat, tunnel or glass
Cornus sericea 'Flaviramea'	Quicker with bottom heat, tunnel or glass
Cosmos atrosanguineus cultivars	Basal cuttings, quicker with bottom heat, tunnel or glass
Cotinus coggygria 'Grace'	Bottom heat and mist
Cotinus coggygria 'Royal Purple'	Bottom heat and mist
Cotoneaster conspicuus 'Decorus'	Quicker with bottom heat, tunnel or glass
Cotoneaster dammeri cultivars	Quicker with bottom heat, tunnel or glass
Cotoneaster franchetii	Quicker with bottom heat, tunnel or glass
Cotoneaster frigidus 'Cornubia'	Quicker with bottom heat, tunnel or glass
Cotoneaster microphyllus	Quicker with bottom heat, tunnel or glass
Cotoneaster salicifolius 'Repens'	Quicker with bottom heat, tunnel or glass
Cotoneaster simonsii	Quicker with bottom heat, tunnel or glass
Cotoneaster × *suecicus* 'Coral Beauty'	Quicker with bottom heat, tunnel or glass
Cotoneaster × *suecicus* 'Skogholm'	Quicker with bottom heat, tunnel or glass

(continued overleaf)

continued

Plant	Propagation Requirements
Cuphea hyssopifolia cultivars	Bottom heat and mist
Delphinium grandiflorum cultivars	Basal cuttings, quicker with bottom heat, tunnel or glass
Delphinium elatum cultivars	Basal cuttings, quicker with bottom heat, tunnel or glass
Deutzia gracilis	Quicker with bottom heat, tunnel or glass
Deutzia gracilis 'Nikko'	Quicker with bottom heat, tunnel or glass
Deutzia × *hybrida* 'Mont Rose'	Quicker with bottom heat, tunnel or glass
Dianthus caryophyllus cultivars	Quicker with bottom heat, tunnel or glass
Dianthus plumarius cultivars	Quicker with bottom heat, tunnel or glass
Diascia elegans cultivars	Bottom heat and tunnel or glasshouse
Escallonia cultivars	Bottom heat and mist
Exochorda × *macrantha* 'The Bride'	Bottom heat and mist
Euonymus alatus	Quicker with bottom heat, tunnel or glass
Fatshedera × *lizei*	Bottom heat and tunnel or glasshouse
Forsythia cultivars	Bottom heat and tunnel or glasshouse
Fuchsia cultivars	Quicker with bottom heat, tunnel or glass
Gaura cultivars	Basal cuttings, quicker with bottom heat, tunnel or glass
Geranium cinereum cultivars	Basal cuttings, quicker with bottom heat, tunnel or glass
Geranium clarkei cultivars	Basal cuttings, quicker with bottom heat, tunnel or glass
Geranium himalayense 'Gravetye'	Basal cuttings, quicker with bottom heat, tunnel or glass
Geranium macrorrhizum cultivars	Basal cuttings, quicker with bottom heat, tunnel or glass
Geranium nodosum	Basal cuttings, quicker with bottom heat, tunnel or glass
Geranium phaeum cultivars	Basal cuttings, quicker with bottom heat, tunnel or glass
Geranium pratense cultivars	Basal cuttings, quicker with bottom heat, tunnel or glass
Geranium psilostemon	Basal cuttings, quicker with bottom heat, tunnel or glass
Geranium sanguineum cultivars	Basal cuttings, quicker with bottom heat, tunnel or glass
Geranium sylvaticum cultivars	Basal cuttings, quicker with bottom heat, tunnel or glass
Geranium × *cantabrigiense* cultivars	Basal cuttings, quicker with bottom heat, tunnel or glass
Geranium × *magnificum* cultivars	Basal cuttings, quicker with bottom heat, tunnel or glass
Geranium × *oxonianum* cultivars	Basal cuttings, quicker with bottom heat, tunnel or glass
Gypsophila paniculata 'Bristol Fairy'	Bottom heat and mist
Hebe albicans	Quicker with bottom heat, tunnel or glass
Hebe cultivars	Quicker with bottom heat, tunnel or glass
Hebe pimeleoides 'Quicksilver'	Quicker with bottom heat, tunnel or glass
Hebe pinguifolia 'Pagei'	Quicker with bottom heat, tunnel or glass
Hebe rakaiensis	Quicker with bottom heat, tunnel or glass
Hedera colchica 'Dentata Variegata'	Quicker with bottom heat, tunnel or glass
Hedera colchica 'Sulphur Heart'	Quicker with bottom heat, tunnel or glass
Hedera helix cultivars	Quicker with bottom heat, tunnel or glass
Helenium cultivars	Quicker with bottom heat, tunnel or glass
Helianthemum cultivars	Quicker with bottom heat, tunnel or glass

(continued overleaf)

continued

Plant	Propagation Requirements
Helichrysum petiolare cultivars	Quicker with bottom heat, tunnel or glass
Heliotropium arborescens cultivars	Quicker with bottom heat, tunnel or glass
Heptacodium miconioides	Bottom heat and mist
Hibiscus syriacus cultivars	Bottom heat and mist
Hippophae rhamnoides	Quicker with bottom heat, tunnel or glass
Humulus lupulus	Quicker with bottom heat, tunnel or glass
Hydrangea anomola ssp. *Petiolaris*	Quicker with bottom heat and mist
Hydrangea arborescens cultivars	Quicker with bottom heat and mist
Hydrangea aspera Villosa Group	Quicker with bottom heat and mist
Hydrangea macrophylla cultivars	Quicker with bottom heat and mist
Hydrangea paniculata cultivars	Quicker with bottom heat and mist
Hydrangea quercifolia	Quicker with bottom heat and mist
Hypericum androsaemum	Quicker with bottom heat, tunnel or glass
Hypericum calycinum	Quicker with bottom heat, tunnel or glass
Hypericum 'Hidcote'	Quicker with bottom heat, tunnel or glass
Hypericum 'Rowallane'	Quicker with bottom heat, tunnel or glass
Hypericum × *moserianum*	Quicker with bottom heat, tunnel or glass
Hypericum × *moserianum* 'Tricolor'	Quicker with bottom heat, tunnel or glass
Hyssopus officinalis	Quicker with bottom heat, tunnel or glass
Impatiens 'New Guinea' cultivars	Quicker with bottom heat, tunnel or glass
Kerria japonica	Quicker with bottom heat, tunnel or glass
Knautia macedonica cultivars	Basal cuttings, quicker with bottom heat, tunnel or glass
Kolkwitzia amabilis 'Pink Cloud'	Quicker with bottom heat, tunnel or glass
Laurentia axillaris cultivars	Quicker with bottom heat, tunnel or glass
Lavandula angustifolia cultivars	Quicker with bottom heat, tunnel or glass
Lavandula stoechas cultivars	Quicker with bottom heat, tunnel or glass
Lavandula × *intermedia* cultivars	Quicker with bottom heat, tunnel or glass
Lavatera cultivars	Quicker with bottom heat, tunnel or glass
Lonicera henryi cultivars	Quicker with bottom heat, tunnel or glass
Lonicera japonica 'Halliana'	Quicker with bottom heat, tunnel or glass
Lonicera ligustrina cultivars	Quicker with bottom heat, tunnel or glass
Lonicera periclymenum cultivars	Quicker with bottom heat, tunnel or glass
Lonicera pileata cultivars	Quicker with bottom heat, tunnel or glass
Lonicera × *americana*	Quicker with bottom heat, tunnel or glass
Lupinus cultivars	Basal cuttings, quicker with bottom heat, tunnel or glass
Lychnis chalcedonica	Basal cuttings, quicker with bottom heat, tunnel or glass
Lychnis flos-cuculi	Basal cuttings, quicker with bottom heat, tunnel or glass
Magnolia liliiflora 'Nigra'	Bottom heat and mist
Magnolia stellata cultivars	Bottom heat and mist
Magnolia × *loebneri* 'Leonard Messel'	Bottom heat and mist

(continued overleaf)

continued

Plant	Propagation Requirements
Magnolia × loebneri 'Merrill'	Bottom heat and mist
Magnolia × soulangeana cultivars	Bottom heat and mist
Mandevilla splendens	Quicker with bottom heat, tunnel or glass
Melianthus major	Basal cuttings, quicker with bottom heat, tunnel or glass
Nemesia cultivars	Quicker with bottom heat, tunnel or glass
Nepeta racemosa cultivars	Quicker with bottom heat, tunnel or glass
Nepeta 'Six Hills Giant'	Quicker with bottom heat, tunnel or glass
Olearia macrodonta	Bottom heat and mist
Olearia × haastii	Bottom heat and mist
Osteospermum cultivars	Quicker with bottom heat, tunnel or glass
Pachysandra terminalis cultivars	Quicker with bottom heat, tunnel or glass
Parthenocissus henryana	Bottom heat and mist
Parthenocissus quinquefolia	Bottom heat and mist
Parthenocissus tricuspidata cultivars	Bottom heat and mist
Passiflora caerulea cultivars	Bottom heat and mist
Pelargonium × peltatum cultivars	Quicker with bottom heat, tunnel or glass
Pelargonium × zonale cultivars	Quicker with bottom heat, tunnel or glass
Penstemon cultivars	Quicker with bottom heat, tunnel or glass
Perovskia atriplicifolia cultivars	Quicker with bottom heat, tunnel or glass
Philadelphus 'Belle Etoile'	Quicker with bottom heat, tunnel or glass
Philadelphus 'Manteau d'Hermine'	Quicker with bottom heat, tunnel or glass
Philadelphus × lemoinei	Quicker with bottom heat, tunnel or glass
Phlox douglasii cultivars	Quicker with bottom heat, tunnel or glass
Phlox paniculata cultivars	Quicker with bottom heat, tunnel or glass
Phlox subulata cultivars	Quicker with bottom heat, tunnel or glass
Physocarpus opulifolius cultivars	Quicker with bottom heat, tunnel or glass
Plectranthus fruticosus cultivars	Quicker with bottom heat, tunnel or glass
Prunus avium cultivars	Bottom heat and mist
Prunus 'Kanzan'	Bottom heat and mist
Prunus padus cultivars	Bottom heat and mist
Prunus sargentii	Bottom heat and mist
Prunus serrula	Bottom heat and mist
Prunus spinosa	Bottom heat and mist
Prunus × yedoensis	Bottom heat and mist
Rhododendron (deciduous azalea)	Bottom heat and mist
Ribes sanguineum cultivars	Quicker with bottom heat, tunnel or glass
Rubus 'Betty Ashburner'	Tunnel or glass
Rubus cockburnianus	Tunnel or glass
Rubus tricolor	Tunnel or glass
Rudbeckia fulgida cultivars	Basal cuttings, quicker with bottom heat, tunnel or glass

(continued overleaf)

continued

Plant	Propagation Requirements
Rudbeckia maxima	Basal cuttings, quicker with bottom heat, tunnel or glass
Salix alba	Tunnel or outdoors
Salix caprea	Tunnel or outdoors
Salix cinerea	Tunnel or outdoors
Salix viminalis	Tunnel or outdoors
Salvia farinacea cultivars	Basal or stem cuttings, quicker with bottom heat, tunnel or glass
Salvia greggii cultivars	Basal or stem cuttings, quicker with bottom heat, tunnel or glass
Salvia nemorosa cultivars	Basal or stem cuttings, quicker with bottom heat, tunnel or glass
Salvia officinalis cultivars	Basal or stem cuttings, quicker with bottom heat, tunnel or glass
Salvia × jamensis cultivars	Basal or stem cuttings, quicker with bottom heat, tunnel or glass
Salvia × superba cultivars	Basal or stem cuttings, quicker with bottom heat, tunnel or glass
Salvia × sylvestris cultivars	Basal or stem cuttings, quicker with bottom heat, tunnel or glass
Sambucus nigra	Quicker with bottom heat, tunnel or glass
Sambucus nigra f. *porphyrophylla* 'Eva'	Quicker with bottom heat, tunnel or glass
Santolina chamaecyparissus cultivars	Quicker with bottom heat, tunnel or glass
Santolina rosmarinifolia ssp. *rosmarinifolia*	Quicker with bottom heat, tunnel or glass
Santolina viridis	Quicker with bottom heat, tunnel or glass
Scabiosa caucasica cultivars	Basal cuttings, quicker with bottom heat, tunnel or glass
Scabiosa 'Pink Mist'	Basal cuttings, quicker with bottom heat, tunnel or glass
Scaevola aemula cultivars	Quicker with bottom heat, tunnel or glass
Sedum Herbstfreude Group	Basal or stem cuttings, quicker with bottom heat, tunnel or glass
Sedum kamtschaticum	Basal or stem cuttings, quicker with bottom heat, tunnel or glass
Sempervivum tectorum	Root offsets
Senecio candidans 'Angels Wings'	Quicker with bottom heat, tunnel or glass
Sequoiadendron giganteum	Bottom heat and mist
Solidago cultivars	Basal cuttings, quicker with bottom heat, tunnel or glass
Sorbus aucuparia cultivars	Bottom heat and mist
Spiraea 'Arguta'	Quicker with bottom heat, tunnel or glass
Spiraea japonica cultivars	Quicker with bottom heat, tunnel or glass
Spiraea nipponica 'Snowmound'	Quicker with bottom heat, tunnel or glass
Spiraea thunbergia	Quicker with bottom heat, tunnel or glass
Staphylea holocarpa	Bottom heat and mist
Succisa pratensis	Basal cuttings, quicker with bottom heat, tunnel or glass
Sutera diffusus cultivars	Bottom heat and mist
Symphoricarpos × chenaultii 'Hancock'	Quicker with bottom heat, tunnel or glass
Symphyotrichum novi-belgii cultivars	Basal cuttings, quicker with bottom heat, tunnel or glass
Syringa meyeri 'Palibin'	Bottom heat and mist
Syringa vulgaris cultivars	Bottom heat and mist
Teucrium chamaedrys	Quicker with bottom heat, tunnel or glass
Teucrium fruticans	Quicker with bottom heat, tunnel or glass

(continued overleaf)

continued

Plant	Propagation Requirements
Thymus citrodorus cultivars	Quicker with bottom heat, tunnel or glass
Thymus 'Doone Valley'	Quicker with bottom heat, tunnel or glass
Thymus 'Jekka'	Quicker with bottom heat, tunnel or glass
Thymus praecox 'Creeping Red'	Quicker with bottom heat, tunnel or glass
Thymus pulegioides 'Archers Gold'	Quicker with bottom heat, tunnel or glass
Thymus serpyllum	Quicker with bottom heat, tunnel or glass
Thymus serpyllum 'Pink Chintz'	Quicker with bottom heat, tunnel or glass
Thymus vulgaris cultivars	Quicker with bottom heat, tunnel or glass
Tilia americana 'Redmond'	Bottom heat and mist
Tilia cordata cultivars	Bottom heat and mist
Ulmus cultivars	Bottom heat and mist
Vaccinium corymbosum cultivars	Quicker with bottom heat, tunnel or glass
Veronica spicata cultivars	Basal cuttings, quicker with bottom heat, tunnel or glass
Viburnum carlesii	Bottom heat and mist
Viburnum lantana	Bottom heat and mist
Viburnum opulus cultivars	Bottom heat and mist
Viburnum plicatum f. *tomentosum* 'Mariesii'	Bottom heat and mist
Viburnum × *bodnantense* 'Dawn'	Bottom heat and mist
Viburnum × *carlcephalum*	Bottom heat and mist
Viola cornuta cultivars	Basal cuttings, quicker with bottom heat, tunnel or glass
Vitis 'Brant'	Quicker with bottom heat, tunnel or glass
Vitis vinifera	Quicker with bottom heat, tunnel or glass
Vitis vinifera 'Purpurea'	Quicker with bottom heat, tunnel or glass
Weigela florida cultivars	Quicker with bottom heat, tunnel or glass
Wisteria floribunda cultivars	Bottom heat and mist
Wisteria sinensis cultivars	Bottom heat and mist

CHAPTER 5

SEMI-RIPE CUTTINGS

What are Semi-Ripe Cuttings?

Semi-ripe cuttings are taken between mid-summer and autumn from the current season's growth on the plant. For evergreen material and conifers, this season can extend into the winter. The material is partially ripe but not woody, and is less flexible than a softwood cutting; the base of the material used should be reasonably firm. Many plants that are difficult to propagate from softwood cuttings are successful as semi-ripe, and it is a widely used method of propagation for a similar range of trees, shrubs, sub-shrubs, alpines and houseplants. The material is still juvenile but can be kept fresh a little longer than softwood cuttings and may need less environmental protection to root in many cases. Semi-ripe cuttings provide more material than softwood, as stem tips, laterals and the bottom sections of the stem can be used.

Make sure that the material used comes from healthy, pest- and disease-free parent plants. Plants propagated by this method may require mist systems and bottom heat, particularly conifers and leafy evergreens, and those taken later in the season. Easily rooted subjects may only need to be under a low polythene tunnel, shade netting or a combination of those, and some are also suitable for direct sticking, reducing the number of potting-on actions needed before they are saleable.

Semi-ripe cuttings root reasonably quickly in the right environment, taking three to eight weeks, depending on the plant and the environment provided. The material should be collected early in the day, using the same collection precautions as for softwood material. The material can also be cold-stored for a day or two at round 4°C.

Euonymnus with semi-ripe material.

Semi-ripe cuttings are usually a little larger than softwood material, but this varies greatly from species to species, and ranges from 7.5 to 15 cm (3–6 in) long. Select material that has no flower bud or remove any flower bud when the cuttings are prepared.

Cuttings should have at least two nodes, and semi-ripe cuttings are usually nodal rather than internodal. The basal cut should be just below a node and the top cut just above, unless the stem tip is being used. Large-leaved plants should have their leaves cut to reduce water loss through transpiration and to enable larger quantities of cuttings to be fitted in to the propagation space. Most semi-ripe cuttings benefit from treatment with rooting hormone and with the base of the cutting wounded.

Leaf-Bud Cuttings

Leaf-bud cuttings are not widely used commercially, except for a few specific examples, such as *Camellia*, *Hedera* and *Clematis*, vines and houseplants. For hardy ornamental nursery stock (HONS) this is usually semi-ripe material, but the type of material – softwood, semi-ripe or hardwood – varies from species to species. Leaf-bud cuttings are cut above the node at the top and the bottom cut is made just above or below a node, depending on whether the species roots best from nodal or internodal cuttings – *Clematis* roots well as internodal leaf-bud cuttings. This leaves one leaf and a leaf bud in the leaf axil. Leaf-bud cuttings produce large quantities of propagules from small amounts of material, so they are worth considering when material is scarce or when demand is outstripping supply. Semi-ripe leaf-bud cuttings should be wounded and rooting hormone treatment applied if necessary, but softwood leaf-bud cuttings may not require this treatment. Leaf-bud cuttings usually require mist and bottom heat for best results.

Equipment

- Secateurs, snips or knife.
- Rooting hormone.
- Compost and cell trays.
- Labels/pens.

Camellia leaf-bud cuttings.

Advantages and disadvantages of semi-ripe cuttings

Advantages of Semi-Ripe Cuttings	Disadvantages of Semi-Ripe Cuttings
Plentiful material	Material needs to be used soon after collection
Ease of rooting	May require a protected environment
Suitable for a wide range of plants	May need over-wintering in a protected environment once rooted
Long potential propagation period	

Taking Semi-Ripe Cuttings

Step 1: Select material.

Step 2: Make two cuttings by cutting just below a node at the base and just above a node at the tip, ensuring a minimum of two nodes.

Step 3: Remove the bottom leaves of plants with larger leaves to aid insertion.

Step 4: Reduce the size of leaves on larger leaved species.

Step 5: Wound the base of the stem, if necessary. Insert into rooting hormone, if necessary.

Step 6: Insert the cuttings into a prepared cell tray. Place in a protected environment.

Taking Leaf-Bud Cuttings – 1

Step 1: Select material.

Step 2: Make two cuttings by cutting just below a node at the base and just above a node at the tip, ensuring a minimum of two nodes. Wound the base of the stem on woodier subjects.

Step 3: Pinch out the top to encourage branching.

Step 4: Insert into rooting hormone, if necessary, and insert into a prepared cell tray. Place in a protected environment.

Taking Leaf-Bud Cuttings – 2

Step 1: Select material.

Step 2: Cut the base just above or below a node, depending on species, so one leaf or leaf pair and leaf axil bud remain. Insert into rooting hormone, if necessary.

Step 3: Insert cuttings into a prepared cell tray. Place in a protected environment.

Materials and Environments

Semi-ripe cuttings may only require a low polythene cover and shading, especially cuttings taken in summer. As with all propagation, good-quality compost, careful irrigation for moist but not over-wet compost, ventilation, humidity and good light levels are essential. Glasshouses or polytunnels are suitable, and heated propagators can be used in the domestic environment. Semi-ripe cuttings taken later in the summer, or through the autumn and winter, will usually need higher levels of protection, which can include mist, bottom heat and heated air temperatures.

Glasshouse or Polytunnel and Bottom Heat

Bottom heat of 18–23°C can be used on more difficult-to-root species. An open mist system can be used, or enclosed mist under low polythene to maintain higher humidity levels. Careful humidity management, especially for larger leaved subjects, reduces water loss through transpiration. Shading is generally required.

Low Polythene without Bottom Heat

Low tunnels without mist are successful for a wide range of subjects, including *Forsythia*, *Philadelphus*, *Spiraea* and *Potentilla*. Low tunnels are cheap to set up and are mobile, so can be used under glass, in polytunnels or outside. Mist systems can be set up under the low tunnel, depending on the species.

Cold Frames

The easiest rooting subjects, such as *Buddleja* and *Hypericum*, can be rooted directly into cold frames, without the need for any extra protection or humidity. This can be straight into cell trays or direct stuck if space allows. Direct sticking of propagules is where one or more cuttings are inserted directly into a larger (possibly final sale size) container, missing out at least one potting on action.

Aftercare and Potting On

As with all propagation, check the cuttings regularly for signs of disease, water stress and also signs of rooting. Remove any dropped leaves and failed cuttings. Apply fungicides as necessary, if required. Monitor the environmental conditions provided and adjust where necessary.

After good root development has taken place, the cuttings can be weaned from their high humidity environment if they have been under mist. This can be done by gradually reducing the frequency and length of misting over seven to ten days and reducing the bottom heat over the same period. Shading can be left, if necessary, especially on cuttings taken in summer.

Potting on into the next stage can be done as soon as there is sufficient root and weaning has taken place to harden the cuttings off. If the cuttings were taken later in the season, especially on deciduous subjects, potting can take place the following spring to reduce over-wintering losses. If the cuttings are not potted, they may require the addition of fertilizer to the root environment.

Protected environments may still be required over winter, either cold tunnels or cold glass, or heated frost protection. The plants at this stage will be vulnerable to frost and overwatering, and other environmental stresses, so careful management of the root and air environment over winter will reduce losses.

Plants to Propagate from Semi-Ripe Cuttings

The difficulty is subjective and may vary according to locality and availability of material. A wide variety of plants may be propagated by more than one method, so whilst semi-ripe cuttings may be an option, some may be more successful by other methods. The conditions suggested do not mean that rooting will not take place without those conditions, but that it may be slower or a lower percentage take.

Rooting hormone should be applied according to manufacturers' recommendations.

Key to difficulty rating

Easy	Roots easily, high-percentage rooting, requires little or no protected environments
Medium	May require some hormone rooting treatment, reasonable rooting percentage, rooting speed and percentage improved with protected environment
Difficult	Difficult to root, low rooting percentage, requires high level of protected environment

Plants to propagate from semi-ripe cuttings and their difficulty rating

Plant	Propagation Requirements
Abelia 'Edward Goucher'	Quicker with bottom heat and mist, tunnel or glass
Abelia grandiflora	Quicker with bottom heat and mist, tunnel or glass
Abelia grandiflora 'Francis Mason'	Quicker with bottom heat and mist, tunnel or glass
Abelia grandiflora 'Gold Spot'	Quicker with bottom heat and mist, tunnel or glass
Abelia schumanii	Quicker with bottom heat and mist, tunnel or glass
Abutilon cultivars	Quicker with bottom heat and mist, tunnel or glass
Acer negundo cultivars	Bottom heat and mist
Acer platanoides cultivars	Bottom heat and mist
Acer pseudoplatanus	Bottom heat and mist
Acer pseudoplatanus 'Brilliantissimum'	Bottom heat and mist
Actinidia kolomikta	Quicker with bottom heat and mist, tunnel or glass
Agastache cultivars	Quicker with bottom heat, tunnel or glass
Ajuga reptans cultivars	Tunnel or glass
Argyranthemum frutescens cultivars	Quicker with bottom heat, tunnel or glass
Artemisia ludoviciana 'Silver Queen'	Quicker with bottom heat, tunnel or glass
Artemisia 'Powis Castle'	Quicker with bottom heat, tunnel or glass
Aucuba japonica cultivars	Quicker with bottom heat and mist, tunnel or glass
Berberis darwinii	Quicker with bottom heat and mist, tunnel or glass
Berberis julianae cultivars	Quicker with bottom heat and mist, tunnel or glass
Berberis thunbergii cultivars	Quicker with bottom heat and mist, tunnel or glass
Berberis verruculosa	Quicker with bottom heat and mist, tunnel or glass
Berberis wilsoniae	Quicker with bottom heat and mist, tunnel or glass
Berberis × *frikartii* 'Amstelveen'	Quicker with bottom heat and mist, tunnel or glass
Berberis × *ottawensis* f. *purpurea* 'Superba'	Quicker with bottom heat and mist, tunnel or glass
Berberis × *stenophylla*	Quicker with bottom heat and mist, tunnel or glass
Bidens ferulifolia cultivars	Quicker with bottom heat, tunnel or glass
Brachyglottis 'Sunshine'	Quicker with bottom heat, tunnel or glass
Buddleja alternifolia	Tunnel or glass
Buddleja davidii cultivars	Tunnel or glass
Buxus microphylla	Quicker with bottom heat and mist, tunnel or glass

(continued overleaf)

continued

Plant	Propagation Requirements
Buxus sempervirens cultivars	Quicker with bottom heat and mist, tunnel or glass
Callicarpa bodinieri 'Profusion'	Quicker with bottom heat, tunnel or glass
Calocephalus brownii	Quicker with bottom heat, tunnel or glass
Camellia japonica cultivars	Bottom heat and mist
Camellia sasanqua cultivars	Bottom heat and mist
Camellia × *williamsii* cultivars	Bottom heat and mist
Caryopteris × *clandonensis* cultivars	Quicker with bottom heat, tunnel or glass
Ceanothus arboreus 'Trewithen Blue'	Quicker with bottom heat and mist, tunnel or glass
Ceanothus 'Autumnal Blue'	Quicker with bottom heat and mist, tunnel or glass
Ceanothus 'Blue Cushion'	Quicker with bottom heat and mist, tunnel or glass
Ceanothus 'Blue Mound'	Quicker with bottom heat and mist, tunnel or glass
Ceanothus 'Concha'	Quicker with bottom heat and mist, tunnel or glass
Ceanothus 'Italian Skies'	Quicker with bottom heat and mist, tunnel or glass
Ceanothus 'Puget Blue'	Quicker with bottom heat and mist, tunnel or glass
Ceanothus thyrsiflorus var. *repens*	Quicker with bottom heat and mist, tunnel or glass
Ceratostigma plumbaginoides	Quicker with bottom heat, tunnel or glass
Ceratostigma willmottianum	Quicker with bottom heat, tunnel or glass
Cercidiphyllum japonicum	Bottom heat and mist
Chaenomeles × *superba* cultivars	Quicker with bottom heat, tunnel or glass
Chamaecyparis lawsoniana cultivars	Quicker with bottom heat, tunnel or glass
Chamaecyparis obtusa cultivars	Quicker with bottom heat, tunnel or glass
Chamaecyparis pisifera cultivars	Quicker with bottom heat, tunnel or glass
Cheiranthus cheiri cultivars	Quicker with bottom heat, tunnel or glass
Choisya ternata	Quicker with bottom heat, tunnel or glass
Choisya ternata 'Sundance'	Quicker with bottom heat, tunnel or glass
Choisya × *dewitteana* 'Aztec Pearl'	Quicker with bottom heat, tunnel or glass
Cistus 'Grayswood Pink'	Quicker with bottom heat, tunnel or glass
Cistus pulverentus	Quicker with bottom heat, tunnel or glass
Cistus purpureus	Quicker with bottom heat, tunnel or glass
Cistus 'Silver Pink'	Quicker with bottom heat, tunnel or glass
Cistus × *dansereaui* 'Decumbens'	Quicker with bottom heat, tunnel or glass
Cistus × *hybridus*	Quicker with bottom heat, tunnel or glass
Cistus × *pulverulentus* 'Sunset'	Quicker with bottom heat, tunnel or glass
Cistus × *purpureus*	Quicker with bottom heat, tunnel or glass
Clematis armandii cultivars	Bottom heat and mist
Clematis large-flowered hybrids	Bottom heat and mist
Clematis integrifolia cultivars	Bottom heat and mist
Clematis montana cultivars	Bottom heat and mist
Clematis viticella cultivars	Bottom heat and mist
Clerodendrum bungei	Quicker with bottom heat, tunnel or glass

(continued overleaf)

continued

Plant	Propagation Requirements
Clerodendrum bungei 'Pink Diamond'	Quicker with bottom heat, tunnel or glass
Coleus × *blumei* cultivars	Quicker with bottom heat, tunnel or glass
Convolvulus cneorum	Quicker with bottom heat, tunnel or glass
Cotoneaster conspicuus 'Decorus'	Quicker with bottom heat, tunnel or glass
Cotoneaster dammeri cultivars	Quicker with bottom heat, tunnel or glass
Cotoneaster franchetii	Quicker with bottom heat, tunnel or glass
Cotoneaster frigidus 'Cornubia'	Quicker with bottom heat, tunnel or glass
Cotoneaster microphyllus	Quicker with bottom heat, tunnel or glass
Cotoneaster salicifolius 'Repens'	Quicker with bottom heat, tunnel or glass
Cotoneaster simonsii	Quicker with bottom heat, tunnel or glass
Cotoneaster × *suecicus* 'Coral Beauty'	Quicker with bottom heat, tunnel or glass
Cotoneaster × *suecicus* 'Skogholm'	Quicker with bottom heat, tunnel or glass
Crinodendron hookerianum	Bottom heat and mist
Cryptomeria japonica cultivars	Quicker with bottom heat, tunnel or glass
Cuphea hyssopifolia cultivars	Quicker with bottom heat, tunnel or glass
Cytisus × *praecox* cultivars	Quicker with bottom heat, tunnel or glass
Daphne odora	Bottom heat and mist
Daphne odora 'Auroomarginata'	Bottom heat and mist
Daphne × *transatlantica* 'Eternal Fragrance'	Bottom heat and mist
Deutzia gracilis	Quicker with bottom heat, tunnel or glass
Deutzia gracilis 'Nikko'	Quicker with bottom heat, tunnel or glass
Deutzia × *hybrida* 'Mont Rose'	Quicker with bottom heat, tunnel or glass
Diascia elegans cultivars	Quicker with bottom heat, tunnel or glass
Elaeagnus pungens 'Maculata'	Quicker with bottom heat, tunnel or glass
Elaeagnus × *ebbingei* cultivars	Quicker with bottom heat, tunnel or glass
Escallonia 'Apple Blossom'	Quicker with bottom heat, tunnel or glass
Escallonia 'Donard Radiance'	Quicker with bottom heat, tunnel or glass
Escallonia 'Donard Seedling'	Quicker with bottom heat, tunnel or glass
Escallonia 'Iveyi'	Quicker with bottom heat, tunnel or glass
Escallonia laevis 'Gold Ellen'	Quicker with bottom heat, tunnel or glass
Escallonia 'Red Hedger'	Quicker with bottom heat, tunnel or glass
Escallonia rubra var. *macrantha*	Quicker with bottom heat, tunnel or glass
Escallonia rubra 'Woodside'	Quicker with bottom heat, tunnel or glass
Euonymus fortunei cultivars	Quicker with bottom heat, tunnel or glass
Euonymus japonicus cultivars	Quicker with bottom heat, tunnel or glass
Fallopia baldschuanica	Quicker with bottom heat, tunnel or glass
Fatshedera × *lizei*	Quicker with bottom heat, tunnel or glass
Fatsia japonica cultivars	Quicker with bottom heat, tunnel or glass
Forsythia cultivars	Quicker with bottom heat, tunnel or glass
Fuchsia cultivars	Quicker with bottom heat, tunnel or glass

(continued overleaf)

continued

Plant	Propagation Requirements
Garrya elliptica	Bottom heat and mist
Gaultheria shallon	Quicker with bottom heat, tunnel or glass
Gaura cultivars	Quicker with bottom heat, tunnel or glass
Gazania cultivars	Quicker with bottom heat, tunnel or glass
Genista hispanica	Quicker with bottom heat, tunnel or glass
Genista lydia	Quicker with bottom heat, tunnel or glass
Glandularia peruviana cultivars	Quicker with bottom heat, tunnel or glass
Grevillea juniperina	Quicker with bottom heat, tunnel or glass
Griselinia littoralis cultivars	Quicker with bottom heat, tunnel or glass
Halesia carolina	Bottom heat and mist
Hebe albicans	Quicker with bottom heat and mist, tunnel or glass
Hebe cultivars	Quicker with bottom heat and mist, tunnel or glass
Hebe pimeleoides 'Quicksilver'	Quicker with bottom heat and mist, tunnel or glass
Hebe pinguifolia 'Pagei'	Quicker with bottom heat and mist, tunnel or glass
Hebe rakaiensis	Quicker with bottom heat and mist, tunnel or glass
Hedera colchica 'Dentata Variegata'	Quicker with bottom heat, tunnel or glass
Hedera colchica 'Sulphur Heart'	Quicker with bottom heat, tunnel or glass
Hedera helix cultivars	Quicker with bottom heat, tunnel or glass
Helichrysum italicum cultivars	Quicker with bottom heat, tunnel or glass
Helichrysum petiolare cultivars	Quicker with bottom heat, tunnel or glass
Heliotropium arborescens cultivars	Quicker with bottom heat, tunnel or glass
Heptacodium miconioides	Bottom heat and mist
Hibiscus syriacus cultivars	Quicker with bottom heat, tunnel or glass
Houttuynia cordata 'Chameleon'	Tunnel or glass
Hydrangea anomola ssp. *petiolaris*	Quicker with bottom heat and mist, tunnel or glass
Hydrangea arborescens cultivars	Quicker with bottom heat and mist, tunnel or glass
Hydrangea aspera Villosa Group	Quicker with bottom heat and mist, tunnel or glass
Hydrangea macrophylla cultivars	Quicker with bottom heat and mist, tunnel or glass
Hydrangea paniculata cultivars	Quicker with bottom heat and mist, tunnel or glass
Hydrangea quercifolia	Quicker with bottom heat and mist, tunnel or glass
Hypericum androsaemum	Quicker with bottom heat, tunnel or glass
Hypericum calycinum	Quicker with bottom heat, tunnel or glass
Hypericum 'Hidcote'	Quicker with bottom heat, tunnel or glass
Hypericum 'Rowallane'	Quicker with bottom heat, tunnel or glass
Hypericum × *moserianum*	Quicker with bottom heat, tunnel or glass
Hypericum × *moserianum* 'Tricolor'	Quicker with bottom heat, tunnel or glass
Iberis sempervirens 'Snowflake'	Quicker with bottom heat, tunnel or glass
Ilex aquifolium cultivars	Quicker with bottom heat, tunnel or glass
Ilex crenata cultivars	Quicker with bottom heat, tunnel or glass
Ilex × *altaclerensis* cultivars	Quicker with bottom heat, tunnel or glass

(continued overleaf)

continued

Plant	Propagation Requirements
Ilex × merserveae cultivars	Quicker with bottom heat, tunnel or glass
Jasminum nudiflorum	Quicker with bottom heat, tunnel or glass
Jasminum officinale cultivars	Quicker with bottom heat and mist, tunnel or glass
Kerria japonica	Quicker with bottom heat, tunnel or glass
Kolkwitzia amabilis 'Pink Cloud'	Quicker with bottom heat, tunnel or glass
Lamium galeobdolon cultivars	Quicker with bottom heat, tunnel or glass
Lamium maculatum cultivars	Quicker with bottom heat, tunnel or glass
Lantana camara cultivars	Quicker with bottom heat, tunnel or glass
Laurus nobilis	Quicker with bottom heat, tunnel or glass
Lavandula angustifolia cultivars	Quicker with bottom heat, tunnel or glass
Lavandula stoechas cultivars	Quicker with bottom heat, tunnel or glass
Lavandula × intermedia cultivars	Quicker with bottom heat, tunnel or glass
Lavatera cultivars	Quicker with bottom heat, tunnel or glass
Ligustrum delavayanum	Quicker with bottom heat, tunnel or glass
Ligustrum lucidum cultivars	Quicker with bottom heat, tunnel or glass
Ligustrum ovalifolium cultivars	Quicker with bottom heat, tunnel or glass
Ligustrum vulgare	Quicker with bottom heat, tunnel or glass
Lithodora diffusa 'Heavenly Blue'	Quicker with bottom heat, tunnel or glass
Lonicera fragrantissima	Quicker with bottom heat, tunnel or glass
Lonicera henryi cultivars	Quicker with bottom heat, tunnel or glass
Lonicera japonica 'Halliana'	Quicker with bottom heat, tunnel or glass
Lonicera ligustrina cultivars	Quicker with bottom heat, tunnel or glass
Lonicera periclymenum cultivars	Quicker with bottom heat, tunnel or glass
Lonicera pileata cultivars	Quicker with bottom heat, tunnel or glass
Lonicera × americana	Quicker with bottom heat, tunnel or glass
Lysimachia nummularia	Quicker with bottom heat, tunnel or glass
Lysimachia nummularia 'Aurea'	Quicker with bottom heat, tunnel or glass
Magnolia grandiflora cultivars	Bottom heat and mist
Magnolia liliiflora 'Nigra'	Bottom heat and mist
Magnolia stellata cultivars	Bottom heat and mist
Magnolia × loebneri 'Leonard Messel'	Bottom heat and mist
Magnolia × loebneri 'Merrill'	Bottom heat and mist
Magnolia × soulangeana cultivars	Bottom heat and mist
Mahonia aquifolium cultivars	Bottom heat and mist
Mahonia eurybracteata ssp. ganpinensis 'Soft Caress'	Bottom heat and mist
Mahonia japonica	Bottom heat and mist
Mahonia × media cultivars	Bottom heat and mist
Mandevilla splendens	Quicker with bottom heat, tunnel or glass
Mentha spicata cultivars	Quicker with bottom heat, tunnel or glass

(continued overleaf)

continued

Plant	Propagation Requirements
Mentha × piperita cultivars	Quicker with bottom heat, tunnel or glass
Muehlenbeckia complexa	Quicker with bottom heat, tunnel or glass
Myrtus communis	Quicker with bottom heat, tunnel or glass
Myrtus communis 'Variegata'	Quicker with bottom heat, tunnel or glass
Nandina domestica cultivars	Quicker with bottom heat, tunnel or glass
Nemesia cultivars	Quicker with bottom heat, tunnel or glass
Nepeta racemose cultivars	Quicker with bottom heat, tunnel or glass
Nepeta 'Six Hills Giant'	Quicker with bottom heat, tunnel or glass
Olea europaea	Bottom heat and mist
Olearia macrodonta	Quicker with bottom heat and mist, tunnel or glass
Olearia × haastii	Quicker with bottom heat and mist, tunnel or glass
Origanum vulgare cultivars	Quicker with bottom heat, tunnel or glass
Osmanthus heterophyllus cultivars	Quicker with bottom heat, tunnel or glass
Osmanthus × burkwoodii	Quicker with bottom heat, tunnel or glass
Osteospermum cultivars	Quicker with bottom heat, tunnel or glass
Pachysandra terminalis cultivars	Quicker with bottom heat, tunnel or glass
Pachysandra terminalis	Quicker with bottom heat, tunnel or glass
Parthenocissus quinquefolia	Quicker with bottom heat, tunnel or glass
Parthenocissus tricuspidate cultivars	Quicker with bottom heat, tunnel or glass
Passiflora caerulea cultivars	Bottom heat and mist
Pelargonium × peltatum cultivars	Quicker with bottom heat, tunnel or glass
Pelargonium × zonale cultivars	Quicker with bottom heat, tunnel or glass
Penstemon cultivars	Quicker with bottom heat, tunnel or glass
Perovskia atriplicifolia cultivars	Quicker with bottom heat, tunnel or glass
Persicaria microcephala 'Chocolate Dragon'	Quicker with bottom heat, tunnel or glass
Persicaria microphylla 'Red Dragon'	Quicker with bottom heat, tunnel or glass
Philadelphus 'Belle Etoile'	Quicker with bottom heat, tunnel or glass
Philadelphus 'Manteau d'Hermine'	Quicker with bottom heat, tunnel or glass
Philadelphus × lemoinei	Quicker with bottom heat, tunnel or glass
Phlomis fruticosa	Tunnel or glass
Phlomis italica	Tunnel or glass
Phlomis russeliana	Tunnel or glass
Photinia × fraseri 'Little Red Robin'	Bottom heat and mist
Photinia × fraseri 'Pink Marble'	Bottom heat and mist
Photinia × fraseri 'Red Robin'	Bottom heat and mist
Physocarpus opulifolius cultivars	Quicker with bottom heat, tunnel or glass
Picea abies cultivars	Bottom heat and mist
Picea glauca cultivars	Bottom heat and mist
Picea omorika cultivars	Bottom heat and mist
Pieris japonica cultivars	Quicker with bottom heat, tunnel or glass

(continued overleaf)

continued

Plant	Propagation Requirements
Pittosporum tenuifolium cultivars	Quicker with bottom heat, tunnel or glass
Pittosporum tobira cultivars	Quicker with bottom heat, tunnel or glass
Plectranthus fruticosus cultivars	Quicker with bottom heat, tunnel or glass
Potentilla fruticosa cultivars	Quicker with bottom heat, tunnel or glass
Prunus laurocerasus cultivars	Quicker with bottom heat, tunnel or glass
Prunus lusitanica cultivars	Quicker with bottom heat, tunnel or glass
Pyracantha coccinea cultivars	Quicker with bottom heat, tunnel or glass
Rhamnus cathartica	Quicker with bottom heat, tunnel or glass
Rhododendron cultivars	Bottom heat and mist
Ribes sanguineum cultivars	Quicker with bottom heat, tunnel or glass
Rosmarinus officinalis cultivars	Quicker with bottom heat, tunnel or glass
Rubus 'Betty Ashburner'	Tunnel or outdoors
Rubus cockburnianus	Tunnel or outdoors
Rubus tricolor	Tunnel or outdoors
Salix alba	Tunnel or outdoors
Salix caprea	Tunnel or outdoors
Salix cinerea	Tunnel or outdoors
Salix viminalis	Tunnel or outdoors
Salvia farinacea cultivars	Quicker with bottom heat, tunnel or glass
Salvia greggii cultivars	Quicker with bottom heat, tunnel or glass
Salvia nemorosa cultivars	Quicker with bottom heat, tunnel or glass
Salvia officinalis cultivars	Quicker with bottom heat, tunnel or glass
Salvia × *jamensis* cultivars	Quicker with bottom heat, tunnel or glass
Salvia × *superba* cultivars	Quicker with bottom heat, tunnel or glass
Salvia × *sylvestris* cultivars	Quicker with bottom heat, tunnel or glass
Sambucus nigra	Quicker with bottom heat, tunnel or glass
Sambucus nigra f. *porphyrophylla* 'Eva'	Quicker with bottom heat, tunnel or glass
Santolina chamaecyparissus cultivars	Quicker with bottom heat, tunnel or glass
Santolina rosmarinifolia ssp. *rosmarinifolia*	Quicker with bottom heat, tunnel or glass
Santolina viridis	Quicker with bottom heat, tunnel or glass
Sarcococca confusa	Quicker with bottom heat, tunnel or glass
Sarcococca hookeriana var. *digyna* 'Purple Stem'	Quicker with bottom heat, tunnel or glass
Sarcococca hookeriana var. *humilis*	Quicker with bottom heat, tunnel or glass
Sarcococca ruscifolia	Quicker with bottom heat, tunnel or glass
Scabiosa caucasica cultivars	Basal cuttings, quicker with bottom heat, tunnel or glass
Senecio candidans 'Angels Wings'	Quicker with bottom heat, tunnel or glass
Sequoiadendron giganteum	Bottom heat and mist
Skimmia japonica 'Kew White'	Quicker with bottom heat, tunnel or glass
Skimmia japonica 'Rubella'	Quicker with bottom heat, tunnel or glass
Skimmia × *confusa* 'Kew Green'	Quicker with bottom heat, tunnel or glass

(continued overleaf)

continued

Plant	Propagation Requirements
Solanum crispum 'Glasnevin'	Quicker with bottom heat, tunnel or glass
Spiraea 'Arguta'	Quicker with bottom heat, tunnel or glass
Spiraea japonica cultivars	Quicker with bottom heat, tunnel or glass
Spiraea nipponica 'Snowmound'	Quicker with bottom heat, tunnel or glass
Spiraea thunbergia	Quicker with bottom heat, tunnel or glass
Staphylea holocarpa	Bottom heat and mist
Sutera diffusus cultivars	Quicker with bottom heat, tunnel or glass
Symphoricarpos × chenaultii 'Hancock'	Quicker with bottom heat, tunnel or glass
Tamarix tetrandra	Quicker with bottom heat, tunnel or glass
Taxus baccata cultivars	Quicker with bottom heat and mist, tunnel or glass
Teucrium chamaedrys	Quicker with bottom heat and mist, tunnel or glass
Teucrium fruticans	Quicker with bottom heat and mist, tunnel or glass
Thuja plicata and culivars	Quicker with bottom heat and mist, tunnel or glass
Thunbergia alata cultivars	Quicker with bottom heat, tunnel or glass
Thymus citrodorus cultivars	Quicker with bottom heat, tunnel or glass
Thymus 'Doone Valley'	Quicker with bottom heat, tunnel or glass
Thymus 'Jekka'	Quicker with bottom heat, tunnel or glass
Thymus praecox 'Creeping Red'	Quicker with bottom heat, tunnel or glass
Thymus pulegioides 'Archers Gold'	Quicker with bottom heat, tunnel or glass
Thymus serpyllum	Quicker with bottom heat, tunnel or glass
Thymus serpyllum 'Pink Chintz'	Quicker with bottom heat, tunnel or glass
Thymus vulgaris cultivars	Quicker with bottom heat, tunnel or glass
Tilia americana cultivars	Bottom heat and mist
Tilia cordata cultivars	Bottom heat and mist
Trachelospermum asiaticum	Bottom heat and mist
Trachelospermum jasminoides cultivars	Bottom heat and mist
Tricyrtis formosana	Quicker with bottom heat, tunnel or glass
Vaccinium corymbosum cultivars	Quicker with bottom heat, tunnel or glass
Viburnum davidii	Quicker with bottom heat and mist, tunnel or glass
Viburnum lantana	Quicker with bottom heat and mist, tunnel or glass
Viburnum odoratissimum	Quicker with bottom heat and mist, tunnel or glass
Viburnum opulus cultivars	Quicker with bottom heat and mist, tunnel or glass
Viburnum rhytidophyllum	Quicker with bottom heat and mist, tunnel or glass
Viburnum sargentii 'Onondaga'	Quicker with bottom heat and mist, tunnel or glass
Viburnum tinus cultivars	Quicker with bottom heat and mist, tunnel or glass
Vinca major cultivars	Tunnel or outdoors
Vinca minor cultivars	Tunnel or outdoors
Vitis vinifera	Quicker with bottom heat, tunnel or glass
Vitis vinifera 'Purpurea'	Quicker with bottom heat, tunnel or glass
Weigela florida cultivars	Quicker with bottom heat, tunnel or glass
x Cuprocyparis leylandii cultivars	Bottom heat and mist

CHAPTER 6

HARDWOOD CUTTINGS

What are Hardwood Cuttings?

Hardwood cuttings are taken between late autumn and mid-winter when the plant is dormant. Deciduous species should be taken several weeks after leaf fall, as the presence of abscisic acid, which causes leaf fall, can inhibit root production. The material usually consists of the previous season's growth, which has become ripe or mature, although there are a few plants, such as *Olea europea* (common olive), that are successful from material that is two years old. There are a wide range of both evergreen and deciduous plants that can be propagated by this method, and many can be rooted using minimal protection, which makes them cheap to produce. Evergreen plants propagated by this method generally require more protection than deciduous subjects.

Fruit, ornamental shrub and rose rootstocks are commonly produced by hardwood cuttings, and whilst rooting may not take place until the following spring, the resulting plants are easily transplanted after rooting, and are often larger than rooted cuttings of softwood material. The cutting material is easy to keep and transport, and can be produced in large quantities.

The cuttings are generally larger than material used for softwood or semi-ripe cuttings, using material that is vigorous – not leggy or weak. Cutting-size depends on species but ranges from 10 to 70 cm (4–28 in) long. The tips of the material should be cut off and discarded as there is often a flower bud at the tip and so the tip will contain fewer resources, which may reduce the chances of the cutting striking successfully.

Cuttings should have at least two nodes, with the basal cut taken just below a node and the top cut just above a node. If it may be difficult to determine which is the top and bottom of the cutting, material with alternate leaf nodes can have the top cut slanted, and the bottom cut straight. Depending on the species, between a half and a third of the cutting should be above the ground or compost, including at least one node. Wounding the cutting – removing a sliver of epidermis from the side of the basal node – and dipping it in rooting hormone is beneficial for most species, both deciduous and evergreen, as wounding exposes more cambium to stimulate cell division and root production. The cambium is a layer of cells that actively divide helping both root production and callousing. The cuttings will then usually callous over at the base, and root production takes place in the spring, depending on species and environmental conditions. Hardwood cuttings that are given a protected environment will root more quickly than those in outdoor beds.

Advantages and disadvantages of hardwood cuttings

Hardwood Cuttings Advantages	Hardwood Cuttings Disadvantages
Low cost	Slow to root and become saleable
Easy to produce	Not suitable for many plants
Easy to transport	Can use valuable space over a long time period
Can be produced without protected environments	

Equipment

- Secateurs or knife.
- Rooting hormone.
- Compost and containers – if using a protected environment.
- Labels/pens.

Taking Hardwood Cuttings

Step 1: Select material.

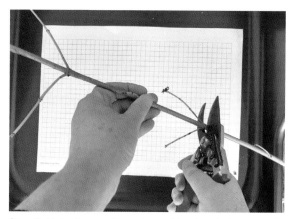

Step 2: Make two cuttings by cutting just below a node at the base and just above a node at the tip, ensuring a minimum of two nodes – make a slanted cut at the top, if necessary.

Step 3: Wound the base to expose the cambium.

Step 4: Insert into rooting hormone in bundles.

Step 5: Insert cuttings into a prepared bed or container in bundles.

Materials and Environments

Hardwood cuttings can be planted in a range of environments, but good light levels, adequate moisture but not over-wet, well-drained soil or compost, and good aeration are always required. Reasonably sheltered conditions are also important for hardwood cuttings going straight into outdoor beds.

Outdoor Beds

Harwood cuttings can be struck directly into prepared outdoor beds, which should be well drained and sheltered from strong winds to prevent desiccation.

Cold Frames or Low Tunnels

Cold frames, cloches or low tunnels can be used to provide protection from low temperatures and excess rain. The other advantage of using this type of protection is that growing media can be used instead of soil, providing good-quality drainage and aeration, where the soil is not suitable.

Glasshouse or Polytunnel and Bottom Heat

Bundles of cuttings can be inserted directly into containers, deep cell trays or beds filled with good-quality cutting compost and placed on bottom heat in glasshouses or polytunnels. This works well for difficult-to-root species, such as some *Juniperus* species, and speeds up the rooting process on easier species. Bottom heat of 18–21°C is generally successful, but some conifer species require up to 24°C to maximize rooting. The air temperature can be ambient for many species, as a heated air environment can cause bud burst before rooting has occurred, but again some harder to root species may require light mist or higher humidity levels. Where harder to root species require a light mist, then fungicide application is recommended, and it is important that the environment does not become too wet.

Aftercare and Potting On

Hardwood cuttings planted directly into outdoor beds or cold frames can be lifted and potted into containers when rooting has taken place, although in outdoor beds the cuttings can be left *in situ* until the following year if space allows, giving the cuttings time to produce a considerable root system. Most species will need to be potted on into the appropriate sized container during the summer after propagation. Potting on before the end of July often has better results than later summer potting.

Keep the areas or containers weed-free and inspect regularly for pests and disease. Good hygiene is important and removal of any fallen leaf material or failed cuttings on a regular basis reduces the occurrence of disease. Regular inspections will also indicate other issues, particularly in protected environments, such as overwatering.

Many species that are suitable for hardwood cuttings are also ideal for 'direct sticking'. This method is good for easy-to-root subjects such as *Salix* species and cultivars. The hardwood cuttings go straight into a 2 ltr pot or a suitable sized container, with two or three cuttings per pot. There is no need to transplant them once they are rooted, and they will be saleable in the container they were rooted in. Additional slow-release fertilizer will need to be added post-rooting, and the reduction in potting cycles makes the plants cheaper to produce; however, they require more space from the initial propagation time.

Plants to Propagate from Hardwood Cuttings

Most plants species that are rooted from hardwood cuttings are easy to root but slow. The application of a protected environment or a protected environment and bottom heat can speed the rooting process, but it may not be necessary unless space is required in the production schedule. The table will only state protected environment and bottom heat if it is necessary for worthwhile rooting percentages. Humidity can be mist or low polythene cover. Rooting hormone should be applied at the manufacturers' recommendations.

Key to difficulty rating

Easy	Roots easily, high-percentage rooting, requires little or no protected environments
Medium	May require some hormone rooting-treatment, reasonable rooting percentage, rooting speed and percentage improved with protected environment and bottom heat
Difficult	Difficult to root, low rooting percentage, requires a high level of protected environment and bottom heat

Plants to propagate from hardwood cuttings and their difficulty rating

Plant	Propagation Requirements
Abies fraseri	Bottom heat and mist
Buddleja alternifolia	Cold frames, cold tunnel, direct sticking, outdoor beds
Buddleja davidii cultivars	Cold frames, cold tunnel, direct sticking, outdoor beds
Campsis radicans	Bottom heat
Campsis × *tagliabuana* 'Madame Galen'	Bottom heat
Caryopteris × *clandonensis* cultivars	Bottom heat
Ceanothus arboreus 'Trewithen Blue'	Bottom heat
Ceanothus 'Autumnal Blue'	Bottom heat
Ceanothus 'Blue Cushion'	Bottom heat
Ceanothus 'Blue Mound'	Bottom heat
Ceanothus 'Concha'	Bottom heat
Ceanothus 'Italian Skies'	Bottom heat
Ceanothus 'Puget Blue'	Bottom heat
Ceanothus thyrsiflorus var. *repens*	Bottom heat
Clematis armandii cultivars	Bottom heat and humidity

(continued overleaf)

continued

Plant	Propagation Requirements
Cornus alba cultivars	Cold frames, cold tunnel, direct sticking, outdoor beds
Cornus sanguinea cultivars	Cold frames, cold tunnel, direct sticking, outdoor beds
Cornus sericea 'Flaviramea'	Cold frames, cold tunnel, direct sticking, outdoor beds
Corylus avellana cultivars	Cold frames, cold tunnel, direct sticking, outdoor beds
Corylus maxima 'Purpurea'	Cold frames, cold tunnel, direct sticking, outdoor beds
Cytisus × *praecox* cultivars	Bottom heat
x *Cuprocyparis leylandii* cultivars	Bottom heat
Deutzia gracilis	Cold frames, cold tunnel, direct sticking, outdoor beds
Deutzia gracilis 'Nikko'	Cold frames, cold tunnel, direct sticking, outdoor beds
Deutzia × *hybrida* 'Mont Rose'	Cold frames, cold tunnel, direct sticking, outdoor beds
Elaeagnus pungens 'Maculata'	Bottom heat
Elaeagnus × *ebbingei* cultivars	Bottom heat
Escallonia 'Apple Blossom'	Bottom heat
Escallonia 'Donard Radiance'	Bottom heat
Escallonia 'Donard Seedling'	Bottom heat
Escallonia 'Iveyi'	Bottom heat
Escallonia laevis 'Gold Ellen'	Bottom heat
Escallonia 'Red Hedger'	Bottom heat
Escallonia rubra var. *macrantha*	Bottom heat
Escallonia rubra 'Woodside'	Bottom heat
Euonymus alatus	Bottom heat
Euonymus japonicus cultivars	Bottom heat
Fallopia baldschuanica	Cold frames, cold tunnel, direct sticking, outdoor beds
Forsythia cultivars	Cold frames, cold tunnel, direct sticking, outdoor beds
Garrya elliptica	Bottom heat and humidity
Genista hispanica	Cold frames, cold tunnel, direct sticking, outdoor beds
Genista lydia	Cold frames, cold tunnel, direct sticking, outdoor beds
Griselinia littoralis cultivars	Bottom heat
Hibiscus syriacus cultivars	Bottom heat
Hydrangea anomola ssp. *petiolaris*	Bottom heat
Hydrangea arborescens cultivars	Bottom heat
Hydrangea aspera Villosa Group	Bottom heat
Hydrangea macrophylla cultivars	Bottom heat
Hydrangea paniculata cultivars	Bottom heat
Hydrangea quercifolia	Bottom heat

(continued overleaf)

continued

Plant	Propagation Requirements
Hypericum androsaemum	Cold frames, cold tunnel, direct sticking, outdoor beds
Hypericum calycinum	Cold frames, cold tunnel, direct sticking, outdoor beds
Hypericum 'Hidcote'	Cold frames, cold tunnel, direct sticking, outdoor beds
Hypericum 'Rowallane'	Cold frames, cold tunnel, direct sticking, outdoor beds
Hypericum × *moserianum*	Cold frames, cold tunnel, direct sticking, outdoor beds
Hypericum × *moserianum* 'Tricolor'	Cold frames, cold tunnel, direct sticking, outdoor beds
Ilex aquifolium cultivars	Bottom heat
Ilex crenata cultivars	Bottom heat
Ilex × *altaclerensis* cultivars	Bottom heat
Ilex × *merserveae* cultivars	Bottom heat
Juniperus communis cultivars	Bottom heat and humidity
Juniperus squamata cultivars	Bottom heat and humidity
Juniperus × *pfitzeriana* cultivars	Bottom heat and humidity
Kerria japonica	Cold frames, cold tunnel, direct sticking, outdoor beds
Ligustrum delavayanum	Cold frames, cold tunnel, direct sticking, outdoor beds
Ligustrum lucidum cultivars	Cold frames, cold tunnel, direct sticking, outdoor beds
Ligustrum ovalifolium cultivars	Cold frames, cold tunnel, direct sticking, outdoor beds
Ligustrum vulgare	Cold frames, cold tunnel, direct sticking, outdoor beds
Lonicera fragrantissima	Cold frames, cold tunnel, direct sticking, outdoor beds
Lonicera ligustrina cultivars	Cold frames, cold tunnel, direct sticking, outdoor beds
Lonicera periclymenum cultivars	Cold frames, cold tunnel, direct sticking, outdoor beds
Lonicera pileata cultivars	Cold frames, cold tunnel, direct sticking, outdoor beds
Mahonia aquifolium cultivars	Bottom heat
Metasequoia glyptostroboides	Bottom heat
Olearia macrodonta	Bottom heat
Parthenocissus henryana	Cold frames, cold tunnel, direct sticking, outdoor beds
Parthenocissus quinquefolia	Cold frames, cold tunnel, direct sticking, outdoor beds
Parthenocissus tricuspidata cultivars	Cold frames, cold tunnel, direct sticking, outdoor beds
Philadelphus 'Belle Etoile'	Cold frames, cold tunnel, direct sticking, outdoor beds
Philadelphus 'Manteau d'Hermine'	Cold frames, cold tunnel, direct sticking, outdoor beds
Philadelphus × *lemoinei*	Cold frames, cold tunnel, direct sticking, outdoor beds
Platanus × *hispanica*	Bottom heat
Populus alba	Cold frames, cold tunnel, direct sticking, outdoor beds
Populus tremula	Cold frames, cold tunnel, direct sticking, outdoor beds
Prunus laurocerasus cultivars	Bottom heat

(continued overleaf)

continued

Plant	Propagation Requirements
Pyracantha coccinea cultivars	Bottom heat
Ribes sanguineum cultivars	Cold frames, cold tunnel, direct sticking, outdoor beds
Rosa bankside	Bottom heat
Rosa canina	Bottom heat
Rosa ground-cover cultivars	Bottom heat
Rosa rugosa	Bottom heat
Rubus 'Betty Ashburner'	Cold frames, cold tunnel, direct sticking, outdoor beds
Rubus cockburnianus	Cold frames, cold tunnel, direct sticking, outdoor beds
Rubus tricolor	Cold frames, cold tunnel, direct sticking, outdoor beds
Salix alba	Cold frames, cold tunnel, direct sticking, outdoor beds
Salix caprea	Cold frames, cold tunnel, direct sticking, outdoor beds
Salix cinerea	Cold frames, cold tunnel, direct sticking, outdoor beds
Salix viminalis	Cold frames, cold tunnel, direct sticking, outdoor beds
Sambucus nigra	Cold frames, cold tunnel, direct sticking, outdoor beds
Sambucus nigra f. *porphyrophylla* 'Eva'	Cold frames, cold tunnel, direct sticking, outdoor beds
Spiraea × *vanhouttei*	Cold frames, cold tunnel, direct sticking, outdoor beds
Symphoricarpos × *chenaultii* 'Hancock'	Cold frames, cold tunnel, direct sticking, outdoor beds
Tamarix tetrandra	Cold frames, cold tunnel, direct sticking, outdoor beds
Thuja plicata cultivars	Bottom heat and mist
Viburnum × *bodnantense*	Cold frames, cold tunnel, direct sticking, outdoor beds
Viburnum × *burkwoodii*	Cold frames, cold tunnel, direct sticking, outdoor beds
Viburnum farreri	Cold frames, cold tunnel, direct sticking, outdoor beds
Viburnum opulus	Cold frames, cold tunnel, direct sticking, outdoor beds
Vitis 'Brant'	Cold frames, cold tunnel, direct sticking, outdoor beds
Vitis coignetiae	Cold frames, cold tunnel, direct sticking, outdoor beds
Vitis vinifera	Cold frames, cold tunnel, direct sticking, outdoor beds
Vitis vinifera 'Purpurea'	Cold frames, cold tunnel, direct sticking, outdoor beds
Weigela florida cultivars	Cold frames, cold tunnel, direct sticking, outdoor beds

CHAPTER 7

ROOT CUTTINGS

What are Root Cuttings?

Root cuttings are taken when the plant is dormant, usually late autumn to late winter, although for some subjects their dormant period may be summer, such as *Primula denticulata*, so root cuttings would be taken in summer. The material should be healthy root from the stock plant, which may be field grown and lifted, or container stock.

There is a select range of trees, shrubs and herbaceous perennials that can be propagated by root cuttings, but availability of material may be an issue commercially. However, if material is available, it is a cheap and effective method of production.

The size of the root cutting can vary hugely and is completely dependent on the root size of the species being propagated. With smaller roots, from herbaceous geraniums or *Eryngium* spp., then they can be between 2.5 and 5 cm (1–2 in) long and laid horizontally on a growing medium in a seed tray or cell tray. They then need to be covered with 1–2 cm $\left(\frac{2}{5} - \frac{4}{5} \text{ in}\right)$ of growing medium, which should be lightly moist. A polythene cover and shade net, if necessary, will prevent the root cuttings from drying out.

Larger and fleshier roots need to be inserted vertically into the growing medium, direct into pots or root trainers. It is vital that cuttings are inserted the correct way up, so the end of the root should be at the bottom, and the top of the root - taken from closest to the crown or main stem of the stock plant – is at the top. The top of the root cutting should have a horizontal cut and the bottom should have a slanted cut. The cuttings of larger roots, such as *Acanthus* or *Syringa*, should be 5–10 cm (2–4 in) long. The cutting should be inserted so that the top of the root is just below the soil surface.

Root cuttings from species that have very large roots, such as *Catalpa bignonioides* or *Liquidamber styraciflua*, can be up to 15 cm (6 in) long, and bundled together vertically, then rooted in pack boxes of either growing medium or a bark/sharp sand mix, prior to being potted on. Again, it is essential that they are the right way up, and the top of the roots should be just below the level of the growing medium.

The speed of rooting and shoot production varies significantly from species to species, and the environment. Rooting hormone is not required for root cuttings. Generally, root cuttings can be potted on in the April/May following propagation. If the material is taken in late winter, then six to eight weeks; although propagation of earlier material will take longer without bottom heat. Root cuttings usually have a high success rate – between 70 and 80 per cent.

Root cuttings of herbaceous perennials.

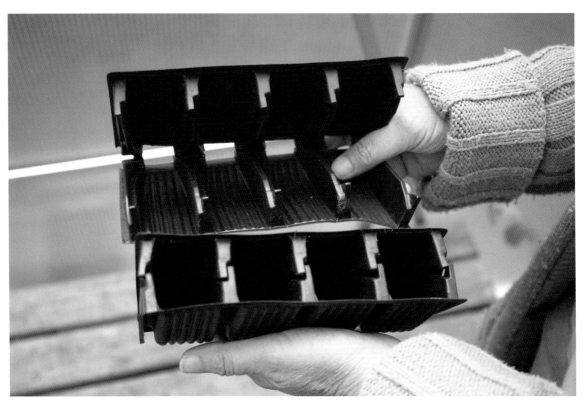

Root trainers (for vertical cuttings).

Advantages and disadvantages of root cuttings

Root Cuttings Advantages	Root Cuttings Disadvantages
Low cost	Sufficient quantities of material may not be available
Easy to produce	Not suitable for many plants
Saleable plants in 12–18 months in most cases	
Can be produced without protected environments	

Equipment

- Secateurs, snips or knife.
- Compost and containers.
- Labels/pens.

Taking Root Cuttings

Step 1: Select material and decide whether it is suitable for horizontal or vertical insertion.

Step 2: Remove suitable lengths of root, ensuring sufficient roots remain on the stock plant.

Step 3: Cut each length of root into sections: thinner roots can be shorter sections, fleshier and larger roots need to be longer. If you wish, make a slanted cut at the top to ensure you place vertical cuttings the right way up.

Step 4: Insert cuttings into a prepared propagation container.

Materials and Environments

Root cuttings need to be protected from excess moisture and drying out, in a sheltered environment. If rooting in cold glass or polytunnels, then covering with polythene and shade net is sufficient.

Cold Frames or Low Tunnels

Cold frames, cloches or low tunnels can be used to provide protection from rain and wind. This type of protection is ideal for easy rooting subjects.

Glasshouse or Polytunnel and Bottom Heat

Most root cuttings root more quickly with bottom heat, although this can also result in very soft top growth, which then needs to be hardened off. Using bottom heat for difficult or slower to root species, such as *Romneya coulteri*, is beneficial, and a bottom heat of 12–15°C is generally successful. They should still be covered with polythene to maintain moisture levels, and good drainage is important to prevent the roots from rotting.

Aftercare and Potting On

Rooted cuttings can be potted on when new roots are showing at the bottom of the container. If the cuttings have been propagated using bottom heat, then hardening off in a cold tunnel, glasshouse or cold-frame will be necessary.

Containers should be kept weed-free and inspected regularly for pests and disease. Remove failed cuttings on a regular basis to reduce the occurrence of disease.

Some species that are suitable for root cuttings are also ideal for 'direct sticking'. This method is good for fleshy rooted, easy to root subjects, such as *Acanthus mollis* cultivars. The root cuttings go straight into a 1 ltr pot or a suitable sized container, with three or four cuttings per pot. There is no need to transplant them once they are rooted, and they will be saleable in the container they were rooted in. Additional slow-release fertilizer will need to be added post-rooting, and the reduction in potting cycles makes the plants cheaper to produce; however, they require more space from the initial propagation time.

Plants to Propagate from Root Cuttings

Most plants that can be propagated by root cuttings root quite easily. Generally, the larger, fleshier roots are inserted vertically, and suggestions for horizontal or vertical are made in the Table.

Key to difficulty rating

Easy	Roots easily, high-percentage rooting, requires little or no protected environment, but should be frost-free
Medium	Rooting speed and percentage improved with protected environment and bottom heat
Difficult	Difficult to root, low-rooting percentage, requires high level of protected environment and bottom heat

Plants to propagate from root cuttings and their difficulty rating

Plant	Propagation Requirements
Acanthus mollis	Vertical
Acanthus spinosus	Vertical
Anemone × hybrida cultivars	Horizontal
Aralia elata	Vertical
Bergenia cordifolia cultivars	Horizontal
Brunnera macrophylla cultivars	Horizontal
Campsis radicans	Vertical
Catalpa bignonioides cultivars	Vertical
Crambe cordifolia	Horizontal
Crambe maritima	Horizontal
Dicentra spectabilis cultivars	Horizontal or vertical
Echinacea purpurea cultivars	Horizontal or vertical
Echinops bannaticus	Horizontal or vertical
Echinops ritro	Horizontal or vertical
Epimedium × perralchicum cultivars	Horizontal or vertical

(continued overleaf)

continued

Plant	Propagation Requirements
Epimedium × *versicolor* cultivars	Horizontal or vertical
Epimedium × *warleyense* cultivars	Horizontal or vertical
Epimedium × *youngianum* cultivars	Horizontal or vertical
Eryngium bourgatii	Horizontal or vertical
Eryngium planum cultivars	Horizontal or vertical
Eryngium variifolium	Horizontal or vertical
Eryngium × *zabelii* 'Big Blue'	Horizontal or vertical
Geranium cinereum cultivars	Horizontal or vertical
Geranium clarkei cultivars	Horizontal or vertical
Geranium himalayense 'Gravetye'	Horizontal or vertical
Geranium macrorrhizum cultivars	Horizontal or vertical
Geranium nodosum	Horizontal or vertical
Geranium phaeum cultivars	Horizontal or vertical
Geranium pratense cultivars	Horizontal or vertical
Geranium psilostemon	Horizontal or vertical
Geranium sanguineum cultivars	Horizontal or vertical
Geranium sylvaticum cultivars	Horizontal or vertical
Geranium × *cantabrigiense* cultivars	Horizontal or vertical
Geranium × *magnificum* cultivars	Horizontal or vertical
Geranium × *oxonianum* cultivars	Horizontal or vertical
Koelreuteria paniculata	Vertical
Macleaya cordata	Horizontal
Mentha spicata cultivars	Horizontal
Mentha × *piperita* cultivars	Horizontal
Papaver orientale cultivars	Horizontal or vertical
Phlox paniculata cultivars	Horizontal or vertical
Pulmonaria cultivars	Horizontal or vertical
Pulsatilla vulgaris cultivars	Horizontal or vertical
Rubus 'Betty Ashburner'	Horizontal or vertical
Rubus cockburnianus	Horizontal or vertical
Rubus tricolor	Horizontal or vertical
Symphytum officinale	Horizontal or vertical
Toona sinensis 'Flamingo'	Vertical
Verbascum chaixii	Horizontal or vertical
Verbascum cultivars	Horizontal or vertical
Wisteria sinensis cultivars	Vertical

CHAPTER 8

LEAF, LEAF-SECTION AND PETIOLE CUTTINGS

What are Leaf and Leaf-Section Cuttings?

A limited number of plants can be propagated from the whole leaf, sections of leaf, or leaf and petiole. Some plants we consider to be houseplants in the UK are routinely propagated by these methods, including *Begonia*, *Streptocarpus*, African violet, *Peperomia* and *Sansevieria*. The cuttings can be taken at any time of the year, if there is healthy, actively growing material and a highly protected environment is available. In the domestic situation, the best time is early spring through to early summer. The leaf or leaf section produces new shoots, buds and roots, and, generally, the original leaf used to make the cutting disintegrates once the new plantlet starts to grow.

Leaf and leaf-section cuttings need bottom heat, mist or high-humidity environments, with well-drained growing media and good ventilation to reduce the potential for disease. In the right environment, rooting and new growth take between two and six weeks, depending on the plant species.

Begonia and *Streptocarpus* can be propagated using the whole leaf. Large-leaved subjects are lightly scored with a sharp knife or scalpel on the underside of the leaf, across the largest veins. The leaf is then laid with the underside of the leaf touching the growing medium. Large leaves may need to be pinned down. The new plants are produced where the veins are cut, and the remainder of the original leaf will disintegrate. Alternatively, large leaves can be cut into smaller sections containing a vein, lightly scored across the vein and then treated as for a whole leaf.

African violets and *Peperomia* can also be propagated using a whole leaf and the leaf petiole. The petiole is inserted upright into the growing medium, so that the base of the leaf is touching the surface, and the new plant will form at the leaf base.

Leaf-blade section cuttings are used on *Sansevieria* and similar subjects. The leaves are cut into sections between 7 and 10 cm (3–4 in) long, and the base of the section is inserted into the growing medium about 2 cm $\left(\frac{4}{5}\,\text{in}\right)$ deep. The section will root and the new plant grows from the base, with the original section being cut off once growth has started, or being left to disintegrate. *Sansevieria trifasciata* var. *laurentii*, the variegated form, will not come true to type by this method as it is a periclinal chimera – which means it has two genetically distinct tissues within the plant.

If the variegated form is required, then it must be propagated by division.

The growing medium for this type of propagation has to be very free-draining, using either perlite or sharp sand mixed with peat-free compost, usually at a 50:50 ratio.

Advantages and disadvantages of leaf, leaf-section and petiole cuttings

Advantages of Leaf Cuttings	Disadvantages of Leaf Cuttings
Lots of propagules from a small amount of material	Material needs to be used very quickly after collection
Ease of rooting	Must have a protected, high-humidity environment
Long potential propagation period	Not suitable for many plants

Equipment

- Scalpel or knife.
- Compost and seed trays or cell trays.
- Labels/pens.
- Protected environment.

Taking Leaf Cuttings

Step 1: Select material.

Step 2: Lightly score across large veins on the underside of the leaf, cut into a section if you are not using the whole leaf.

Step 3: Lay leaves on the growing medium, underside down.

Step 4: Pin down using wire or small stones. Place in a protected environment.

Taking Leaf-Petiole Cuttings

Step 1: Cut at base of the petiole so you have a whole leaf with petiole attached.

Step 2: Make a cut at the bottom of the petiole.

Step 3: Insert the petiole into the growing medium so that the leaf is upright – use a pencil or dibber to make the hole and place in a protected environment.

Taking Leaf-Blade or Leaf-Section Cuttings

Sansevieria.

Step 1: Select material – cut a whole leaf blade to the base of the plant.

Step 2: Cut the leaf into sections – 7–10 cm (3–4 in) long.

Step 3: Insert sections 2 cm $\left(\frac{4}{5}\text{ in}\right)$ deep into prepared seed tray – making sure that the base of the section goes into the compost – the cutting must be the right way up – and place in protected environment.

Materials and Environments

The compost mix, as previously stated, should be sharply draining. A mix of peat-free, low-nutrient compost and perlite or sharp sand is ideal. Vermiculite can also be used as a top layer, as it provides warm, moist but well-drained contact between the leaf and the growing medium, which helps to reduce the incidence of disease.

Glasshouse or Polytunnel and Bottom Heat

Bottom heat of 18–23°C is required, with an ambient air temperature in a similar range. High humidity is also needed, so use a closed mist system or low polythene on hoops over a heated bench. The ventilation and drainage are crucial, as the leaves can quickly deteriorate if there is too much moisture in the compost. Shading will be required if cuttings are taken in summer and placed under glass.

Aftercare and Potting On

Check the cuttings regularly for signs of disease, water stress and new plantlets showing. Remove any failed cuttings. Apply fungicides as necessary, if required. Monitor the environmental conditions provided and adjust where necessary.

After good shoot and root development have taken place, the cuttings can be weaned from their high-humidity environment if they have been under mist. This can be done by gradually reducing the

frequency and length of misting over seven to ten days and reducing the bottom heat over the same period. Shading can be left if necessary, especially on cuttings taken in summer.

Potting on into the next stage can be done as soon as there is sufficient growth of both roots and propagules, and weaning has taken place to harden the cuttings off.

Protected environments will still be required, but humidity levels can be reduced. As many of the subjects suitable for this type of propagation are considered to be houseplants in the northern hemisphere, minimum temperatures suitable for the species must be maintained.

Plants to Propagate from Leaf Section, Leaf Petiole or Stem Section Cuttings

All the plants in this category will require bottom heat and a protected environment. This can be a domestic propagator or similar, but providing heat and humidity is important, and will result in higher percentage of rooting, and also reduce the chances of the leaf or leaf section rotting off. All the plants listed in the Table will root reasonably easily if the right environment is provided.

Key to difficulty rating

Easy	Roots easily, high-percentage rooting, requires little or no protected environment, but should be frost-free
Medium	Rooting speed and percentage improved with protected environment and bottom heat
Difficult	Difficult to root, low rooting percentage, requires high level of protected environment and bottom heat

Plants to propagate from leaf section, leaf petiole or stem section cuttings and their difficulty rating

Plant	Propagation Requirements
Begonia rex cultivars	Leaf and leaf section
Crassula	Leaf cutting
Echeveria	Leaf cutting
Eucomis	Leaf section
Gloxinia	Leaf and leaf section
Kalanchoe	Leaf cutting
Peperomia	Leaf petiole
Sansevieria	Leaf section
Sedum rubrum	Leaf cutting
Streptocarpus (African violets)	Leaf petiole
Streptocarpus cultivars	Leaf and leaf section
Veltheimia	Leaf section

CHAPTER 9

LAYERING

What is Layering?

Layering can take various forms, but essentially it is a method by which new plants are produced whilst still attached to the parent plant. It takes advantage of methods used naturally by certain plants to colonize and reproduce in their environments. Plants that have a natural tendency to sucker, produce runners or off-sets, are stoloniferous – having a stem that grows along the ground producing roots and shoots at nodes – or rhizomatous – an underground stem that produces roots and shoots – these can be propa-gated by layering. It is less commonly used as a commercial form of propagation, except on specific subjects that may be difficult to root by other meth-ods, as it is labour intensive and can take up a lot of space, as well as requiring stock plants to be main-tained for the purposes of layering, generally in field-stock beds.

Mound Layering or Stooling

This is used commercially on fruit rootstocks and a few other woody trees and shrubs, such as *Cotinus, Viburnum bodnantense* and *Cornus* species. The new shoots are cut back annually to just above ground level during dormancy, and soil or substrate is mounded up, in a similar way to 'earthing up' potatoes, as new shoots are produced. Once the shoots are up to 12.5 cm (5 in) (depending on species), then soil is mounded halfway up the new shoot. This process can be repeated two or three times during the growing season, until the shoots have a covering of between 15 and 20 cm (6–8 in). The new shoots develop roots at the base of the mound and can be cut away at the end of the growing season as rooted cuttings. They can then either be containerized, dispatched directly to customers or transplanted.

Simple Layering

Stems from the previous season's growth (one-year-old wood) are bent over from the parent plant to the ground and a section of the stem is covered in soil or substrate, then pegged down, leaving the tip of the stem showing. This is usually done in spring to early summer while the plants are actively growing. The stems produce roots at the covered section, and can be separated the following autumn or winter and transplanted or containerized. This is a useful method for woody plants with a suckering habit, such as *Corylus* species, *Syringa* species and *Tilia* species. Simple layering is also a good method for creeping plants, such as *Ajuga*, *Lamium*, *Thymus* and heathers.

Compound Layering

The entire stem is laid horizontally and covered in soil and pegged down. This is similar to simple layering, but produces more plants, as a new shoot and root is formed at each node point along the stem. This can be used on plants such as grapevines, which have long stems with lots of nodes. The pegging down of the stem usually takes place during the dormant period, before active growth starts. The new plants are then separated and transplanted or containerized in the autumn.

Serpentine Layering

This is a similar technique to compound layering, but the shoot is pegged down in a series of 'S' shapes. It works well on plants that have long stems that are not naturally very straight, such as *Wisteria* or *Philodendron*.

Air Layering

Air layering is a technique used mainly on tropical plants, which are used as houseplants or conservatory plants in the UK. The previous season's growth, about one-year-old, are selected, and a sliver of bark about 2 cm $\left(\frac{4}{5}\text{ in}\right)$ long is removed at a node to make a wound. The wound can then be treated with a rooting hormone, if required. The wound is then enclosed in a growing medium, such as sphagnum moss, and wrapped in clear poly-thene or cling film. The ends can be taped up with waterproof tape. Most plants propagated by this method require a protected environment, with high humidity and minimum temperatures suitable for the parent plant, and shading is also beneficial. Many *Ficus* species can be propagated in this way, as well as *Monstera* and *Draceana*. In more temperate regions, *Magnolia grandiflora* and other woody species can be air layered outside.

Equipment

- Knife for wounding – depending on species.
- Wire for pegging into the ground.
- Loose soil or substrate for mounding.
- Moss or similar substrate, cling film and tape for air layering.

Advantages and disadvantages of layering

Layering Advantages	Layering Disadvantages
Easy to root	Requires planned stock grounds and parent stock management
Does not usually require protected environments	Takes up a lot of space
Large quantities can be produced	Labour intensive
Useful for subjects that are otherwise difficult to root	Not suitable for many plants

Simple Layering

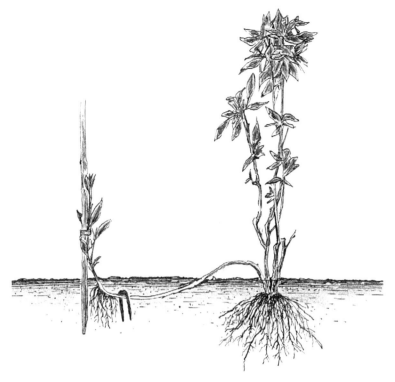

Diagram of simple layering.

Step 1: Select material from the previous season's growth.
Step 2: Bend over from the parent plant, forming a 'U'-shape.
Step 3: Peg down at the bottom of the 'U' and cover with soil or substrate.
Step 4: Leave the tip exposed.

Serpentine and Compound Layering

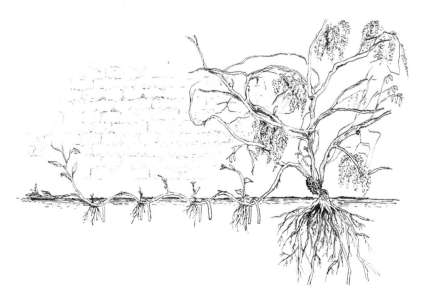

Diagram of serpentine layering.

Step 1: Select material from the previous season's growth.
Step 2: Place horizontally on the ground in a series of 'S' shapes or a straight line.
Step 3: Peg down between each node.
Step 4: Cover with soil or substrate at each node.

Materials and Environments

Unless layering tropical plants, layering does not require protected environments. The purpose is to use field-grown stock plants that are managed for this specific propagation method, particularly fruit rootstocks. There may be a requirement for extra substrate when mound layering. Field irrigation may be required whilst rooting takes place, as periods of drought will have a detrimental effect on the new plants, as well as on the parent plant's ability to produce new shoots for the following year.

Aftercare and Potting On

Propagules raised from layering are usually potted on in the autumn after rooting has occurred and, as they are generally field grown, they can be containerized or transplanted to field rows. When grown in this way they do not need to be moved to a protected environment.

Plants to Propagate by Layering

Layering plants is no longer a widely used commercial technique, as it requires a lot of space and can take some time to produce saleable plants, but for domestic purposes it can be a useful method if equipment and resources for other techniques are not available.

Key to difficulty rating

Easy	Roots easily, high-percentage rooting, requires little or no protected environment
Medium	Rooting speed and percentage slower than easy subjects, start layering in spring if possible
Difficult	Can be difficult, slow and erratic to root, start layering in spring if possible

Plants to propagate by layering and their difficulty rating

Plant
Abeliophyllum distichum
Actinidia kolomikta
Akebia quinata
Amelanchier canadensis cultivars
Amelanchier lamarckii cultivars
Campanula carpatica cultivars
Chaenomeles × superba cultivars
Clematis armandii cultivars
Clematis large flowered hybrids
Clematis integrifolia cultivars
Clematis montana cultivars
Clematis vitalba
Clematis viticella cultivars
Cornus alba cultivars
Cornus sanguinea cultivars
Cornus sericea 'Flaviramea'
Corylus avellana cultivars
Corylus maxima 'Purpurea'

Plant
Cotinus coggygria 'Grace'
Cotinus coggygria 'Royal Purple'
Cotoneaster conspicuus 'Decorus'
Cotoneaster dammeri cultivars
Cotoneaster franchetii
Cotoneaster frigidus 'Cornubia'
Cotoneaster microphyllus
Cotoneaster salicifolius 'Repens'
Cotoneaster simonsii
Cotoneaster × suecicus 'Coral Beauty'
Cotoneaster × suecicus 'Skogholm'
Daphne odora
Daphne odora 'Aureomarginata'
Daphne × transatlantica Eternal Fragrance
Dianthus plumarius cultivars
Fallopia baldschuanica
Fatshedera × lizei
Forsythia cultivars

(continued overleaf)

continued

Plant
Hedera colchica 'Dentata Variegata'
Hedera colchica 'Sulphur Heart'
Hedera helix cultivars
Humulus lupulus
Hydrangea anomola ssp. *petiolaris*
Hydrangea arborescens cultivars
Hydrangea quercifolia
Hypericum androsaemum
Hypericum calycinum
Hypericum 'Hidcote'
Hypericum 'Rowallane'
Hypericum × *moserianum*
Hypericum × *moserianum* 'Tricolor'
Jasminum nudiflorum
Jasminum officinale cultivars
Kerria japonica
Kolkwitzia amabilis 'Pink Cloud'
Lamium galeobdolon cultivars
Lamium maculatum cultivars
Lonicera fragrantissima
Lonicera henryi cultivars
Lonicera japonica 'Halliana'
Lonicera ligustrina cultivars
Lonicera periclymenum cultivars
Lonicera pileate cultivars
Lonicera × *americana*
Lysimachia nummularia
Lysimachia nummularia 'Aurea'
Magnolia grandiflora cultivars
Mentha spicata cultivars

Plant
Mentha × *piperita* cultivars
Nepeta racemosa cultivars
Nepeta 'Six Hills Giant'
Origanum vulgare cultivars
Pachysandra terminalis cultivars
Parthenocissus henryana
Parthenocissus quinquefolia
Parthenocissus tricuspidata cultivars
Passiflora caerulea cultivars
Populus alba
Populus tremula
Rhododendron cultivars
Rubus 'Betty Ashburner'
Rubus cockburnianus
Rubus tricolor
Thymus citrodorus cultivars
Thymus 'Doone Valley'
Thymus 'Jekka'
Thymus praecox 'Creeping Red'
Thymus pulegioides 'Archers Gold'
Thymus serpyllum
Thymus serpyllum 'Pink Chintz'
Thymus vulgaris cultivars
Trachelospermum asiaticum
Trachelospermum jasminoides cultivars
Viburnum carlesii
Vitis 'Brant'
Vitis coignetiae
Vitis vinifera
Vitis vinifera 'Purpurea'

CHAPTER 10

DIVISION

What is Division?

Division is a method of propagation that can be practiced on a wide variety of subjects, particularly herbaceous perennials, ornamental grasses and many alpine plants. Plants that are clump-forming, matt-forming or produce rhizomes are ideal. The crowns can be split when they are dormant, although there are many exceptions to this, for plants such as iris need to be divided after flowering. Other early flowering herbaceous perennials also divide well as soon as flowering has finished. Many herbaceous perennials and other subjects suitable for division, such as sedums, respond well to dividing in the spring, when growth has actively started.

Increasing stock by division is dependent on having a suitable quantity of stock material, and commercial nurseries often use bought-in plug plants rather than dividing existing stock. Division is also a labour-intensive method of propagation, which requires knowledge of individual species, as there can be significant differences between dividing an *Agapanthus* or a *Saxifraga*.

Hardy plants that are propagated by division will rarely need an intensively protected environment. Sections for division should be taken from the outer parts of the parent plant, rather than the older, centre of the crown. Each section will have some roots and dormant buds, which can produce new, saleable plants. Divisions can also be cold-stored successfully to fit in with a potting schedule.

Advantages and disadvantages of division

Division Advantages	Division Disadvantages
Already rooted, easy to grow on	Labour intensive
Economical if stock plants are available	Stock plants require valuable nursery space
Do not generally require high levels of protected environment	Not suitable for woody subjects
Suitable for a wide range of herbaceous and alpine plants	

Equipment

- Knife or can be done with a spade for larger crowns or home gardening.
- Container.
- Good-quality growing compost.
- Labels/pens.

Step 1: Select material – either field grown and lifted, or container-grown.

Step 2: Remove old foliage and stems to clean up the crown.

Step 3: Cut sections with roots and buds from the outer sphere of the plant, leaving the crown intact.

Step 4: Pot into a suitable container straight away and place in a cold tunnel or similar.

Materials and Environments

Divisions of hardy subjects will need careful irrigation, but generally do not require a heated environment, which makes them an economical way of increasing stock.

Aftercare and Potting On

Once the divisions are potted, they can be grown on until saleable or until they require potting on if a larger plant is required. Check regularly for any failures and remove them. Shading may be required for late spring and summer divisions, to ensure temperatures do not get too high, which can cause young plants to dry out very quickly.

Plants to Propagate by Division

Most plants that are suitable for division, will have good success rates if the section has enough root and dormant buds, so all the plants listed in the Table should all be reasonably easy if the parent plant has suitable growth.

Key to difficulty rating

Easy	Roots easily, high-percentage rooting, requires little or no protected environment, but should be frost-free
Medium	Rooting speed and percentage improved with protected environment and bottom heat
Difficult	Difficult to root, low rooting percentage, requires high level of protected environment and bottom heat

Plants to propagate by division and their difficulty rating

Plants
Acaena microphylla cultivars
Acanthus mollis
Acanthus spinosus
Achillea filipendulina cultivars
Achillea millefolium cultivars
Achillea ptarmica 'The Pearl'
Aconitum carmichaelii cultivars
Aconitum napellus cultivars
Acorus calamus cultivars
Acorus gramineus 'Ogon'
Actaea simplex Atropurpurea Group cultivars
Actaea simplex cultivars
Agapanthus africanus cultivars
Agapanthus campanulatus cultivars
Agastache cultivars
Agastache foeniculum
Ajuga reptans cultivars
Alchemilla mollis
Allium schoenoprasum
Allium tuberosum
Alstroemeria cultivars
Anaphalis triplinervis cultivars
Anemanthele lessoniana
Anemone coronaria cultivars
Anemone × hybrida cultivars
Angelonia angustifolia cultivars
Arabis caucasica cultivars
Armeria maritima cultivars
Artemisia ludoviciana 'Silver Queen'
Aruncus dioicus
Asplenium scolopendrium
Aster × frikartii cultivars
Astilbe chinensis cultivars
Astilbe × arendsii cultivars
Astrantia major cultivars
Athyrium filix-femina
Athyrium niponicum cultivars
Aubrieta × hybrida cultivars
Baptisia australis
Begonia × benariensis cultivars

Plants
Begonia × tuberhybrida cultivars
Bergenia cordifolia cultivars
Brunnera macrophylla cultivars
Calamagrostis × acutiflora cultivars
Calamintha nepeta cultivars
Calla palustris
Campanula carpatica cultivars
Campanula glomerata cultivars
Campanula lactiflora cultivars
Campanula persicifolia cultivars
Campanula portenschlagiana cultivars
Canna indica cultivars
Carex brunnea cultivars
Carex buchananii cultivars
Carex comans cultivars
Carex elata cultivars
Carex flagellifera cultivars
Carex hachijoensis cultivars
Carex morrowii cultivars
Carex testacea cultivars
Cephalaria gigantea
Cheilanthes lanosa
Cirsium rivulare 'Atropurpureum'
Coreopsis verticillate cultivars
Cornus canadensis
Cortaderia selloana cultivars
Crambe cordifolia
Crambe maritima
Crocosmia cultivars
Cynara cardunculus
Delphinium grandiflorum cultivars
Deschampsia cespitosa cultivars
Deschampsia flexuosa cultivars
Dicentra formosa
Dicentra spectabilis cultivars
Digitalis × mertonensis
Digitalis parviflora
Doronicum orientale cultivars
Dryopteris affinis cultivars
Dryopteris cycadina

(continued overleaf)

continued

Plants
Dryopteris erythrosora cultivars
Dryopteris filix-mas cultivars
Dryopteris wallichiana
Echinacea purpurea cultivars
Echinops bannaticus
Echinops ritro
Epimedium × *perralchicum* cultivars
Epimedium × *versicolor* cultivars
Epimedium × *warleyense* cultivars
Epimedium × *youngianum* cultivars
Eryngium agavifolium
Euphorbia amygdaloides var robbiae
Euphorbia characias subsp wulfenii
Euphorbia palustris
Euphorbia polychroma
Euphorbia shillingii
Fargesia murieliae 'Simba'
Fargesia nitida cultivars
Fargesia robusta cultivars
Festuca glauca cultivars
Filipendula rubra
Filipendula ulmaria
Gaillardia × *grandiflora* cultivars
Geranium cinereum cultivars
Geranium clarkei cultivars
Geranium himalayense 'Gravetye'
Geranium macrorrhizum cultivars
Geranium nodosum
Geranium phaeum cultivars
Geranium pratense cultivars
Geranium psilostemon
Geranium sanguineum cultivars
Geranium sylvaticum cultivars
Geranium × *cantabrigiense* cultivars
Geranium × *magnificum* cultivars
Geranium × *oxonianum* cultivars
Geum 'Borisii'
Geum chiloense cultivars
Gunnera manicata
Helenium cultivars
Helianthus decapetala
Helleborus niger
Helleborus × *orientalis* cultivars
Hemerocallis cultivars
Heuchera cultivars
Heucherella cultivars

Plants
Hosta cultivars
Houttuynia cordata 'Chameleon'
Imperata cylindrica 'Rubra'
Iris foetidissima
Iris germanica cultivars
Iris pseudacorus
Iris sibirica cultivars
Juncus effusus cultivars
Kalimeris incisa cultivars
Knautia macedonica cultivars
Kniphofia cultivars
Koeleria glauca cultivars
Lamium galeobdolon cultivars
Lamium maculatum cultivars
Leucanthemum × *superbum* cultivars
Levisticum officinale
Lewisia × *hybrida* cultivars
Liatris spicata
Ligularia dentata 'Desdemona'
Limonium platyphyllum
Liriope muscari cultivars
Lobelia speciosa cultivars
Lupinus cultivars
Luzula sylvatica cultivars
Lychnis chalcedonica
Lychnis flos-cuculi
Lysimachia clethroides
Lysimachia punctata
Lythrum salicaria cultivars
Macleaya cordata
Matteuccia struthiopteris
Melianthus major
Melica altissima 'Atropurpurea'
Mentha spicata cultivars
Mentha × *piperita* cultivars
Milium effusum 'Aureum'
Miscanthus sinensis cultivars
Miscanthus × *giganteus*
Molinia caerulea cultivars
Monarda cultivars
Mukdenia rossii cultivars
Myosotis sylvatica cultivars
Nepeta racemosa cultivars
Nepeta 'Six Hills Giant'
Ophiopogon planiscapus 'Kokuryu'
Origanum vulgare cultivars

(continued overleaf)

continued

Plants
Osmunda regalis
Pachysandra terminalis cultivars
Panicum virgatum cultivars
Pennisetum alopecuroides cultivars
Pennisetum glaucum cultivars
Pennisetum orientale
Pennisetum villosum cultivars
Persicaria affinis 'Superba'
Persicaria amplexicaulis
Persicaria bistorta cultivars
Persicaria microcephala 'Chocolate Dragon'
Persicaria microphylla 'Red Dragon'
Phlomis fruticosa
Phlomis italica
Phlomis russeliana
Phlox paniculata cultivars
Phlox subulata cultivars
Phormium tenax cultivars
Phyllostachys aurea
Phyllostachys nigra
Physostegia virginiana cultivars
Polemonium caeruleum cultivars
Polypodium vulgare
Polystichum aculeatum
Polystichum munitum
Polystichum polyblepharum
Polystichum setiferum cultivars
Polystichum tsus-simense
Primula elatior cultivars
Primula obconica cultivars
Primula veris cultivars
Primula vialii
Primula vulgaris cultivars
Pseudosasa japonica
Pulmonaria cultivars
Pulsatilla vulgaris cultivars
Rheum palmatum var. *tanguticum*
Rudbeckia fulgida cultivars
Rudbeckia maxima
Ruscus aculeatus
Salvia × *superba* cultivars
Salvia × *sylvestris* cultivars
Sanguisorba canadensis
Sanguisorba menziesii

Plants
Sanguisorba officinalis
Sasa veitchii
Saxifraga × *arendsii* cultivars
Scabiosa caucasica cultivars
Scabiosa 'Pink Mist'
Schizachyrium scoparium 'Blaze'
Sedum Herbstfreude Group
Sedum kamtschaticum var. *kamtschaticum* 'Weihenstephaner Gold'
Sedum spurium cultivars
Senecio candidans 'Angels Wings'
Sidalcea cultivars
Sisyrinchium striatum
Solidago 'Goldkind'
Sporobolus heterolepis
Stachys byzantina cultivars
Stipa gigantea
Stipa tenuissima cultivars
Symphyotrichum novi-belgii cultivars
Symphytum officinale
Tellima grandiflora
Thalictrum delavayi
Thymus citrodorus cultivars
Thymus 'Doone Valley'
Thymus 'Jekka'
Thymus praecox 'Creeping Red'
Thymus pulegioides 'Archer's Gold'
Thymus serpyllum
Thymus serpyllum 'Pink Chintz'
Thymus vulgaris cultivars
Tiarella cordifolia cultivars
Tiarella wherryi
Tradescantia Andersoniana Group
Tricyrtis formosana
Trollius europaeus
Trollius chinensis 'Golden Queen'
Tulbaghia violacea
Uncinia rubra
Veronica spicata cultivars
Veronicastrum virginicum 'Fascination'
Vinca major cultivars
Vinca minor cultivars
Viola cornuta cultivars

CHAPTER 11

GRAFTING AND BUDDING

What is Grafting and Budding?

Grafting and budding are the most highly skilled forms of propagation, and there are many different techniques within this. This chapter will discuss the basic methods, but to go into detail about each different form of grafting would be another book in itself and, indeed, there are a few books dedicated to this subject.

Grafting and budding are the propagation method by which a rootstock has another plant joined to it, so that the required cultivar, e.g. a *Wisteria* cultivar, grows on the rootstock of another plant. The reasons for this are to combine the superior qualities of the scion – the cultivar – with qualities provided by the rootstock. The scion may be free-flowering, fruit heavily, be difficult to propagate by other methods or a 'standard' plant where the scion is grafted on to the rootstock at a specific height to produce a specific form, such as a weeping standard. The rootstock may control size and vigour – dwarfing fruit rootstocks – as well as resistance to disease or resilience to environmental conditions. Combining these attributes can produce valuable ornamental plants, commercial fruit trees and other subjects that could be saleable more quickly, flower at a younger age or fruit earlier.

Budding is essentially the same as grafting, but single buds from the required cultivar are inserted on to the rootstock. 'T'-budding on roses is carried out in mid to late summer when the rootstock and the bud material are in active growth. 'T'-budding involves lifting a flap of the bark of the rootstock to insert the bud into – so the plants must be in active growth for this to be done easily. Chip budding is used on fruit trees, and is the same principle, but can be carried out in spring and autumn.

The basic principle for successful grafting is to match the vascular cambium of the scion to the vascular cambium of the rootstock. Vascular cambium is the tissue that forms new phloem and xylem, and will enable the graft union to combine effectively. The graft union needs to be held together so that the rootstock can supply the scion with water and nutrients.

Graft compatibility – the compatibility of the rootstock and the scion – are essential. This is often a rootstock of the same species as the cultivar, but similar species can also be used. Occasionally, plants may be compatible for grafting on to a different genus – *Syringa vulgaris* cultivars used to be grafted on to *Ligustrum* rootstocks – but whilst the graft may hold for a few years, in this case the rootstock often grew too vigorously and became the main plant, with the scion dying off.

Advantages and disadvantages of grafting and budding

Advantages of Grafting or Budding	Disadvantages of Grafting or Budding
Saleable plant quickly for subjects that are hard to propagate by other methods	Material needs to be used quickly after collection or cold stored
Rootstock confers benefits on the scion, such as vigour, and resilience to pests or disease	Requires highly skilled labour
Some subjects will flower at a younger age than if propagated by other methods	Needs careful management
Suitable for a wide range of plants	May require a protected environment – more expensive
High-value plants produced	Labour intensive

Grafting and budding are carried out on woody ornamentals, such as trees, shrubs, fruit trees, standards, vines and climbers, but increasingly grafting is being used as a commercial technique on vegetable plants, such as curcubits and tomatoes.

Grafting and budding can be carried out on open-ground plants – field grafting – or on container-grown plants – bench grafting. Budding is widely used on field-grown roses, where the rootstocks are lined out and grown in nursery fields, and then budded whilst still *in situ*, during the growing season. They are then lifted the following winter, and either sold bare root or containerized for sale.

Timing of the grafting operation can vary widely between species, and in the case of vegetables can be done almost all year round. Grafting of many woody ornamentals is carried out during the dormant season but may also be carried out in mid to late summer.

This chapter will cover four basic techniques: whip or splice graft, whip and tongue graft, side veneer graft and T-budding.

Equipment

- Propagation knife, grafting knife or budding knife.
- Containerized rootstocks for bench grafting – open-ground rootstocks for field grafting.
- Scion material – one-year-old or current season's growth.
- Grafting ties, tape, patches or wax.
- Heated benches providing basal heat of 18–20°C for bench grafts.
- Frost-free air temperature for winter bench grafts.
- Low polythene tunnels over heated benches for summer bench grafts.
- Shading for summer bench grafts.
- Labels/pens.

Whip or Splice Graft

The whip or splice graft is an example of apical grafting and is one of the simplest grafting methods, requiring only two cuts. The scion and the rootstock must be of similar diameter; a slanted cut is made across the top of the rootstock and a corresponding cut from the base of the scion. The scion cut is then matched to the rootstock and they are tied together.

Making a Whip or Splice Graft Bench Grafting on to a Container-Grown Rootstock

Step 1: Select scion material and appropriate rootstock – they should be of a similar diameter. Cut the rootstock just above a bud at the required height, this will vary depending on the subject – but is usually between 7.5 and 15 cm (3–6 in).

Step 2: Make a slanted cut starting approximately 2.5–3 cm $\left(1-1\frac{1}{4}\text{ in}\right)$ below the top of the rootstock to the tip of the rootstock.

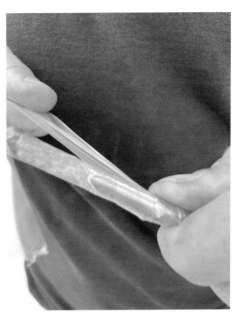

Step 4: Place together and tie using grafting ties or bands.

Step 3: Make a corresponding slanted cut from the base of the scion to 2.3–3 cm $\left(1-1\frac{1}{4}\text{ in}\right)$ up the stem – the cuts should match.

Step 5: Wax if required – usually on deciduous material – and place in a protected environment.

Whip and Tongue Graft

The whip and tongue graft is useful for thinner material, as well as woodier subjects, and can have higher success rates, as there is a greater area of contact between the scion and the rootstock. The cuts are made as for a whip graft, then a second downward cut is made in the rootstock, from a little below the top to the base of the initial cut. A corresponding second cut is made in the scion, which creates an interlinking 'tongue'. The rootstock and scion can then be fitted together, which gives a larger area of secure contact, and often a stronger graft union.

Making a Whip and Tongue Graft

Step 2: Cut the scion material to appropriate lengths – usually between 12.5 and 20 cm (5–9 in).

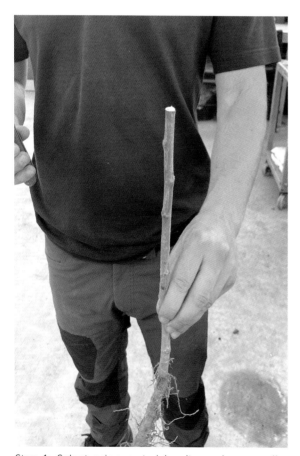

Step 1: Select scion material – it can be a smaller diameter than the field-grown rootstock. Cut the rootstock just above a bud at the required height – this will vary depending on the subject – but usually between 7.5 and 15 cm (3–6 in).

Step 3: Make a slanted cut starting approximately 2.5–3 cm $\left(1–1\frac{1}{4}\text{ in}\right)$ below the top of the rootstock to the tip of the rootstock. Make a corresponding slanted cut from the base of the scion to 2.3–3 cm $\left(1–1\frac{1}{4}\text{ in}\right)$ up the stem – the cuts should match.

Step 4: Make a downward slice – the tongue – halfway down the cut on the rootstock.

Step 6. Insert the scion on to the rootstock, so that the 'tongues' wedge together.

Step 5: Make a corresponding slice in the cut on the scion.

Step 7: Tie the graft using grafting ties or bands – the advantage of a whip and tongue graft is that it will hold together without a tie – so the tie can be put on by another operator rather than the person doing the grafting.

Side Veneer Graft

A side veneer graft can be used on a wider range of species than whip and tongue grafting, and is useful for subjects such as dwarf conifers. The rootstocks are usually at the liner stage (where the rootstock is well-rooted, usually at 9 cm pot size); a cut is made at the base of the scion and a corresponding cut toward the bottom of the rootstock. The rootstock can be left growing and cut back gradually as the scion 'takes'.

Making a Side Veneer Graft for Bench Grafting

Step 1: Select scion material – it can be a smaller diameter than the rootstock – and cut the scion material to appropriate lengths – usually between 12.5 and 20 cm (5–9 in).

Step 2: Make a shallow, sliced cut into the side of the rootstock at the required height – depending on species, between 5 and 15 cm (2–6 in).

Step 3: Take a longer, shallow slice down to the first cut, to leave a 'tongue' at the bottom.

Step 4: Make a corresponding shallow slice into the bottom of the scion so that the cambium matches.

Step 5: Wedge the scion into the 'tongue' on the rootstock.

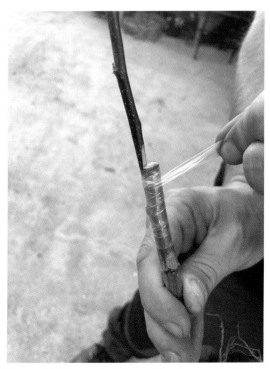

Step 6: Tie the graft using grafting ties or bands, wax if necessary and place in a protected environment.

Chip Budding

Chip budding is generally used on field-grown stock.

Step 1: Remove leaves from scion (bud stick) material.

Step 2: Make a shallow cut from approximately 2 cm $\left(\frac{4}{5}\text{in}\right)$ above a healthy bud and remove the bud; buds should be kept moist and shaded at all times.

Step 3: Clean the stem the rootstock to the required height – do not cut back.

Step 4: Make a shallow vertical cut, 3–4 cm $\left(1–1\frac{1}{2}\ \text{in}\right)$ long, in the rootstock at the required height – ground level for roses but between 10 and 20 cm (4–8 in) for ornamental subjects.

Step 5: Insert the bud on to the rootstock.

Step 6: Tie the graft using grafting ties, bands or bud patches.

Materials and Environments

Bench-grafted material should not be overwatered, the growing media in the container kept just moist. Bench grafts may require varying levels of protection, whilst field-grafted plants do not, other than weed and pest- or disease-free environments.

Glasshouse or Polytunnel and Bottom Heat

Winter bench grafts may require bottom heat, but they also need a cool ambient temperature. This is to stimulate rootstock activity. A basal temperature of 18–20°C, under cold glass or polythene is usually sufficient; however, the air temperature may need boosting during very cold periods. The air temperature should always be frost-free. Ensuring good ventilation also helps to reduce temperature fluctuations that might force the graft into growth too early.

Low Polythene without Bottom Heat

Summer bench-grafted plants can be kept under low tunnels to maintain humidity and will not usually require base heating. As summer grafts will have foliage on the scion material and rootstock, some foliage can be cut back on the scion, if necessary. Shading may be required to prevent temperatures becoming too high. The growing media will need to be kept moist and not allowed to dry out.

Aftercare and Potting On

Field-grafted or budded plants do not require a protected environment, but care must be taken to maintain them once the graft or bud unions have been successful. Some ties and patches are biodegradable, but those that are not must be removed when the graft union has successfully formed, otherwise the rootstock and graft union will be constricted, which can lead to graft failure or fungal disease at the graft union.

The rootstocks of field-grafted or budded plants should be cut back – 'headed back' – to just above the union, the following winter, and any suckers removed as the appear. The scion shoots should be cut back by half if they grow away too strongly or to maintain a particular shape.

Bench grafts need careful water management, with irrigation increasing once the scion is putting on growth. The graft union should be callused over after approximately six to eight weeks, and the ties will need removing if they are not biodegradable. The plants should be weaned off the bottom heat, but kept under glass or tunnels.

Checking regularly for signs of pests or disease, particularly fungal diseases that might occur around the graft union, is essential, and any failed grafts should be removed.

Plants to Propagate from Grafting or Budding

With all the different grafting and budding methods, it is worth practicing the actual technique on material that is available in enough quantity for the skill to be honed. *Salix alba* cultivars are good to practice on, as the material is usually plentiful and is available in different stem colours, so it makes the distinction between 'rootstock' and 'scion' very clear. *Cornus alba* cultivars can also be used for the same reason. Practicing on materials from this type of coppiced plant – plants that are cut back hard each spring for stem colour or leaf colour – means the propagator can become more proficient at making the cuts involved without wasting scarce or expensive propagation material. It will also give confidence in the process of tying and binding the rootstock and scion together. When practicing cut lengths of material, don't worry that your practice rootstock doesn't have any roots, mastering the technique is the important thing. Alternatively, you can root *Salix* as semi-ripe or hardwood cuttings, and then use these as rootstocks to practice on.

All grafting and budding is a skilled and difficult process. The Table gives commonly used methods of grafting or budding for different plants, but this will vary from nursery to nursery. Some plants on this list would not normally be propagated by grafting except as top-worked standards, e.g. holly.

Plants to propagate from grafting or budding and their difficulty rating

Difficult	This type of propagation requires a high level of skill and knowledge of different types of plants and techniques. Some may be field grafted or budded and require little in the way of protected environments, but others need bottom heat, protection and controlled environments. All have been rated as difficult, as the type of rootstock, timing, scion material quality, skill of propagator and environment are all crucial to successful grafting and budding.

Plant	Propagation Requirements
Abies fraseri cultivars	Side veneer graft
Abies koreana	Side veneer graft
Abies nordmaniana	Side veneer graft
Acer capillipes cultivars	Side veneer graft
Acer cappadocicum cultivars	Side veneer graft
Acer davidii cultivars	Side veneer graft
Acer griseum cultivars	Side veneer graft
Acer japonicum cultivars	Side veneer graft
Acer negundo cultivars	Side veneer graft
Acer palmatum cultivars	Side veneer graft
Acer platanoides cultivars	Side veneer graft
Acer pseudoplatanus 'Brilliantissimum'	Side veneer graft
Aesculus hippocastanum cultivars	Whip or splice graft
Betula nigra cultivars	Whip or splice graft
Betula pendula cultivars	Whip or splice graft
Betula utilis var. *jacquemontii*	Whip or splice graft
Camellia japonica cultivars	Whip or splice graft
Camellia sasanqua cultivars	Whip or splice graft
Camellia × *williamsii* cultivars	Whip or splice graft
Carpinus betulus cultivar	Whip or splice graft
Catalpa bignonioides cultivars	T-budding
Cercis siliquastrum 'Forest Pansy'	Whip or splice graft
Chamaecyparis lawsoniana cultivars	Side veneer graft
Chamaecyparis obtusa cultivars	Side veneer graft
Chamaecyparis pisifera cultivars	Side veneer graft
Cornus controversa cultivars	Whip or splice graft
Cornus kousa cultivars	Whip or splice graft
Crataegus laevigata cultivars	T-budding
Crataegus persimilis 'Prunifolia Splendens'	T-budding
Crataegus × *lavalleei*	T-budding
Daphne odora	Side veneer graft
Daphne odora 'Aureomarginata'	Side veneer graft
Daphne × *transatlantica* 'Eternal Fragrance'	Side veneer graft
Fagus sylvatica cultivars	Side veneer graft
Gleditsia triacanthos cultivars	Whip and tongue graft
Hamamelis × *intermedia* cultivars	Chip budding
Hamamelis mollis cultivars	Chip budding
Hibiscus syriacus cultivars	Whip or splice graft
Ilex aquifolium cultivars	Chip budding
Ilex crenata cultivars	Chip budding
Ilex × *altaclerensis* cultivars	Chip budding
Ilex × *merserveae* cultivars	Chip budding
Juniperus communis cultivars	Side veneer graft
Juniperus scopulorum cultivars	Side veneer graft
Liquidambar styraciflua cultivars	Whip or splice graft
Liriodendron tulipifera	Whip or splice graft
Magnolia grandiflora cultivars	Whip or splice graft
Magnolia liliiflora 'Nigra'	Side veneer graft
Magnolia stellata cultivars	Side veneer graft

(continued overleaf)

continued

Plant	Propagation Requirements
Magnolia × *loebneri* 'Leonard Messel'	Side veneer graft
Magnolia × *loebneri* 'Merrill'	Side veneer graft
Magnolia × *soulangeana* cultivars	Side veneer graft
Malus domestica cultivars	T-budding or chip budding
Malus sylvestris	T-budding or chip budding
Malus tschonoskii	T-budding or chip budding
Malus × *moerlandsii* 'Profusion'	T-budding or chip budding
Malus × *robusta* 'Red Sentinel'	T-budding or chip budding
Malus × *zumi* var. *calocarpa* 'Golden Hornet'	T-budding or chip budding
Mespilus germanica	Chip budding
Paeonia lactiflora cultivars	Apical wedge graft
Picea abies cultivars	Side veneer graft
Picea glauca cultivars	Side veneer graft
Picea omorika cultivars	Side veneer graft
Pinus nigra cultivars	Side veneer graft
Pinus strobus cultivars	Side veneer graft
Pinus sylvestris cultivars	Side veneer graft
Prunus avium cultivars	Whip and tongue graft
Prunus 'Kanzan'	Whip and tongue graft
Prunus 'Kiku-shidare-zakura'	T-budding or chip budding
Prunus padus cultivars	Whip and tongue graft
Prunus sargentii cultivars	Whip and tongue graft
Prunus serrula cultivars	Whip and tongue graft
Pyrus calleryana 'Chanticleer'	Whip and tongue graft
Pyrus communis cultivars	Whip and tongue graft
Pyrus salicifolia 'Pendula'	T-budding or chip budding
Rhododendron cultivars	Side veneer graft
Rhododendron (deciduous azalea)	Side veneer graft
Rosa climber cultivars	T-budding
Rosa floribunda cultivars	T-budding
Rosa ground cover cultivars	T-budding
Rosa hybrid tea cultivars	T-budding
Rosa rambler cultivars	T-budding
Rosa shrub rose cultivars	T-budding
Sorbus aria 'Lutescens'	Chip budding
Sorbus aucuparia cultivars	Chip budding
Syringa vulgaris cultivars	Whip or splice graft
Taxus baccata cultivars	Side veneer graft
Thuja plicata cultivars	Side veneer graft
Tilia americana 'Redmond'	T-budding or chip budding
Tilia cordata cultivars	T-budding or chip budding
Tilia henryana	T-budding or chip budding
Tilia × *euchlora*	T-budding or chip budding
Viburnum carlesii	Side veneer graft
Wisteria floribunda cultivars	Apical wedge graft
Wisteria sinensis cultivars	Apical wedge graft

CHAPTER 12

BULB PROPAGATION

What are Bulbs?

Bulb is a term that is often misapplied to corms, tubers, rhizomes and other forms of modified storage organs. These often produce bulblets or offsets that can be used to propagate them. True bulbs are usually mono-cotyledons, with the exception of some *Oxalis* species. All of these types of storage organ allow the plant to withstand difficult growing conditions, such as drought or a cold winter, but the plants can also propagate themselves vegetatively from these organs.

Bulb

A bulb is an underground storage organ that consists of a central (apical) bud and overlapping scale leaves. This central bud contains the immature foliage and flower of the plant, which emerge during the growing season, usually drawing resources from the scale leaves.

Examples include *Narcissus*, tulips, onions and hyacinth.

Corm

A corm is a swollen underground stem containing food reserves. The corm has nodes, which from new stems, and roots are produced from the base. The corm is replaced at the end of each growing season by a new corm.

Examples include gladioli, crocus and freesia.

Tubers

Tubers are similar to corms and are also underground storge organs. The tuber has distinct buds or 'eyes' and is replaced each year.

Examples include potato and anemone.

Root Tuber

A root tuber is a swollen root that produces stems at the top and roots at the bottom, initially using reserves from the tuber. They can be biennial or perennial.

Examples include *Dahlia* and *Hemerocallis*.

Stem Tuber

A stem tuber is a swollen stem that is also a storage organ, and they are usually perennial, often increasing in size each year.

Examples include tuberous *Begonia* and *Cyclamen*.

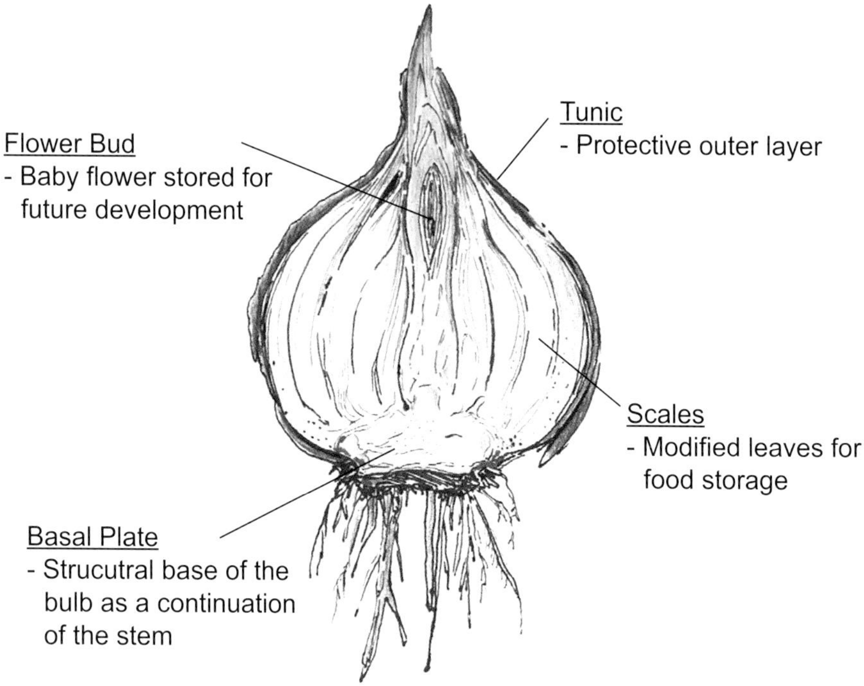

Diagram of a bulb.

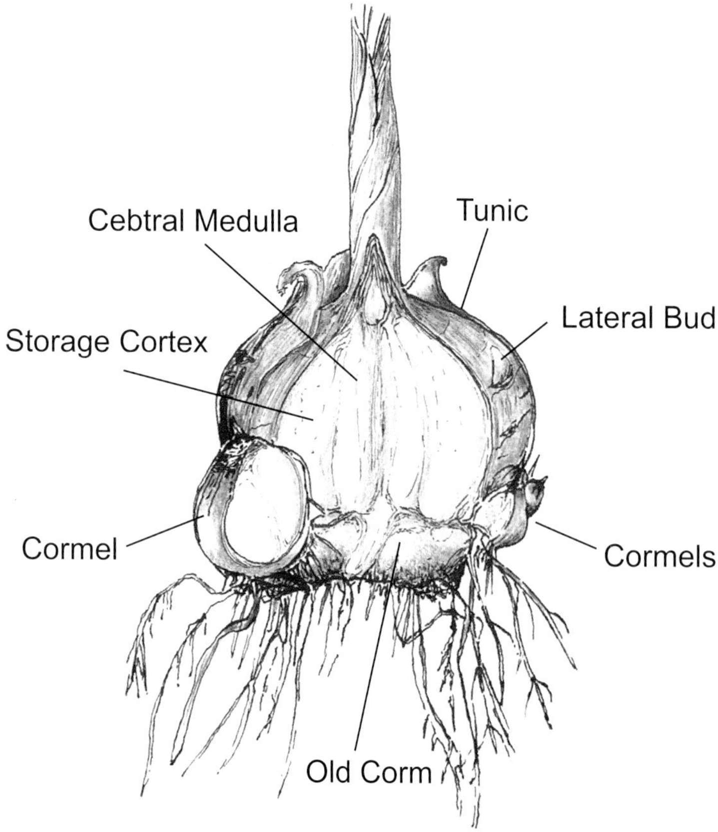

Flower Bud
- Baby flower stored for
  future development

Tunic
- Protective outer layer

Scales
- Modified leaves for
  food storage

Basal Plate
- Strucutral base of the
  bulb as a continuation
  of the stem

Cebtral Medulla

Tunic

Storage Cortex

Lateral Bud

Cormel

Cormels

Old Corm

Diagram of a corn.

Diagram of a tuber.

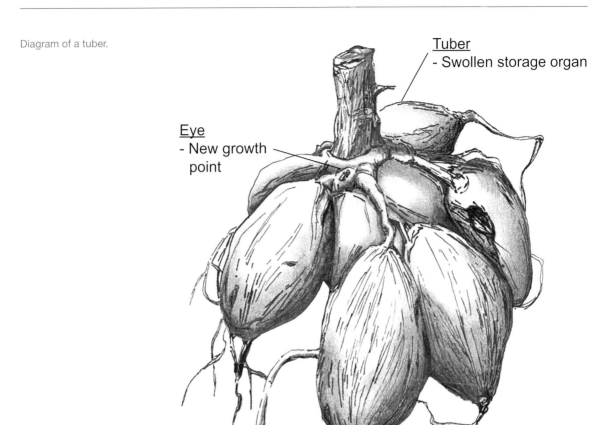

Eye
- New growth
  point

Tuber
- Swollen storage organ

Rhizome

A rhizome is a modified stem that grows at or just below ground level, horizontally.

Examples include bamboo, *Iris*, *Convallaria* and *Canna*.

Bulb and Modified Stem Propagation Techniques

Bulbs and modified storage organs can be propagated by division, offsets, micropropagation and, in some cases, stem cuttings.

Offsets

Offsets are smaller bulbs produced by, but still attached to, the main bulb. These are easily removed and in some plants, such as *Narcissus*, are produced quickly by the parent bulb, enabling the offsets to be used in commercial production. The offsets may take several seasons to become large enough to flower, and are often left on the parent bulb to increase in size. Other types of bulb, such as *Hippeastrum*, are much slower in producing offsets, so commercial propagation by this method is rare.

Scaling

Scaling is where scales are removed from the parent bulb and grown on individually. This can be done once the parent bulb has become dormant, with the outer one or two layers of scales removed for growing on. It is a good method for bulbs such as lillies, which have layers of scales. The scales produce between two and five bulblets, so it can be a useful way of increasing stock rapidly. The scales should be removed as close to the base as possible and placed in a clear plastic bag containing moist vermiculite, keeping as much air in

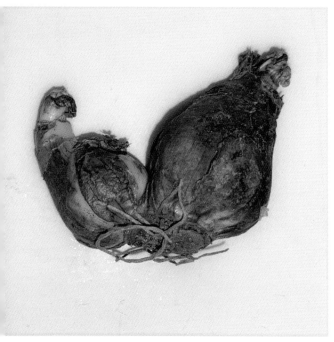

An offset.

Bulb Chipping

Bulb chipping is where the dormant parent bulb is cut into vertical sections, as if you were cutting an apple into pieces. Each section should contain a piece of the basal plate of the bulb and cut into roughly equal sections, depending on the size of the bulb. They can then be planted into a suitable growing medium, deep enough so that the tip of the bulb section is just showing at the surface, and with a bottom heat of 15–20°C. They will produce new bulblets at the basal plate. *Hippeastrum* and *Nerines* can be propagated by this method, as can many other bulbs.

Sections

Corms, tubers and rhizomes can be propagated by sectioning. A corm can be cut into sections and, as long as there is a bud on each section, they will become new corms. Corms generally increase naturally each year too. Tubers can also be divided, sections containing a bud and some root being cut off planted or stored – dahlias are often propagated in this way.

Cuttings

Cuttings can be taken from the new growth of tubers in the same way as for basal cuttings (*see* Chapter 4).

the bag as possible, before closing it. Leave the bag in a warm, dark place – around 20°C – for about six weeks. Check after six weeks and the bulblets should have formed at the base of the scales; these can then be potted on individually. Remove the old scales if they are soft or starting to become soft, but if they are healthy, they can be left on. It is worth considering using a fungicide before the scales are placed in the bag or container, as fungal disease is a common cause of failure.

Alternatively, plant the scales in trays of moist vermiculite, to about half their length, on bottom heat at around 20°C. Check after three weeks, but it is usually between three and six weeks before bulblets are produced, which can then be potted on.

Bulb to Propagate

The Table gives a common method of propagation for the plant, but they may also be able to be propagated from seed, division or offsets, as well as the method stated.

Key to difficulty rating

Easy	Roots easily, high-percentage rooting, requires little or no protected environment
Medium	Rooting speed and percentage slower than easy subjects, better results with bottom heat and some protection
Difficult	Difficult to root, low rooting percentage, requires high level of protected environment and bottom heat

Bulbs to propagate and their difficulty rating

Plant	Propagation Requirements
Allium hollandicum cultivars	Bulb chipping
Amaryllis belladonna	Bulb chipping
Begonia (tuberous)	Sections
Caladium cultivars	Sections
Crocosmia cultivars	Sections
Cyclamen cultivars	Sections
Dahlia cultivars	Tuber division
Eranthis hyemalis	Sections
Fritillaria cultivars	Chipping or scaling
Galanthus cultivars	Chipping or scaling
Gladiolus cultivars	Sections
Hippeastrum cultivars	Chipping
Hyacinthus cultivars	Chipping or scaling
Iris Juno Group	Bulb chipping
Lilium cultivars	Chipping or scaling
Narcissus cultivars	Chipping or scaling
Nerine cultivars	Chipping
Scilla cultivars	Chipping
Sternbergia lutea	Chipping

CHAPTER 13

MICROPROPAGATION

What is Micropropagation?

Micropropagation, or plant-tissue culture, is the propagation of pieces of plant tissue in a highly controlled and sterile environment – very small pieces of plant tissue, usually from sections of the plant that have vigorous growing tips that will actively divide. Micropropagation is an important method of commercial propagation and produces millions of plants each year, although it still only accounts for a small proportion of plants propagated vegetatively. Plants propagated by micropropagation range from orchids to bulbs, hardy nursery stock and herbaceous perennials. It can be particularly useful for plants that are difficult or slow to propagate by other methods, including some rhododendron species, orchids and ferns. Many orchids, such as *Phalaeonopsis* and *Cymbidiums* are freely available and significantly cheaper because of their production through micropropagation.

The material can be taken at any time of year that the parent plant is actively growing, and the parent plants are usually container grown, kept in optimum conditions. Vigorous juvenile growth from well-managed stock plants is essential. High levels of hygiene, as well as healthy, pest- and disease-free material, are essential. *Heuchera*, *Hosta* and other popular herbaceous perennials are very successful using micropropagation, and this enables new cultivars to be increased at a much faster rate than traditional propagation methods, such as division.

A sterile laboratory is required for the process, and the equipment needed is expensive to set up, and the labour costs can be significant. The propagules are called explants and are sterilized in alcohol and bleach solutions before being placed in the growing culture. Laminar airflow cabinets are used to pass filtered air over the explants to remove microbes and dust particles. The growing culture usually consists of agar jelly with added nutrients and hormones, which vary depending on the species being propagated and the stage of propagation. Higher cytokinin levels are important in the first stage for shoot production, and higher auxin levels in the following stage for root production. The growing culture is in sterile containers or test tubes, in which the explants are placed.

The containers are then placed in a growing cabinet or a grow room, at temperatures of between 20 and 25°C, although again this may vary depending on species. Light at this stage can be low-intensity fluorescent or LED lighting.

Once in the grow cabinet or room, the explants increase quickly; more propagules are taken from the new shoots and inserted into separate growing media

Micropropagation of blueberry.

Growing blueberry plants in sterile conditions by *in vitro* technology.

promote root production. They continue to then be grown on in the grow room or cabinet.

Weaning

Weaning micropropagated plants into a different growing medium and environment is a complex and difficult stage of tissue culture. The plants are potted into cell trays or small pots, and need to be kept in a highly controlled environment – stable temperatures and humidity levels – to start the weaning process. Micropropagated plants don't tend to have waxy cuticles, and the stomata are often permanently open, which means the plants lose water easily and quickly at this stage. This can also mean that they are susceptible to fungal diseases, so overwatering can be as problematic as underwatering and low humidity. Bottom heat is required, shading during months when light levels are high and protection for several

containers (subcultures). This continues until the required quantity of propagules has been achieved.

The next stage is to induce rooting, and individual plants are now removed and placed in new growing media – agar jelly usually with increased auxin levels to

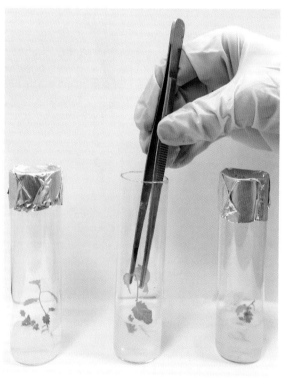

Graftage of micro plants in a laboratory of biotechnology for *in vitro* cultivating in test tube.

Advantages and disadvantages of micropropagation

Micropropagation Advantages	Micropropagation Disadvantages
Large quantities of plants can be produced from stock plants in comparison to traditional methods of propagation	Expensive and specialized equipment required
Bulks up stock of new cultivars for retail sales	High labour costs
Increases stock of endangered or difficult to propagate plants	Weaning needs highly protected and controlled environments and management
Production of pest-, disease- and virus-free plants	
Increase stock of plants slow to propagate by other methods	
All year round production	

weeks with levels of protection gradually being reduced so the hardened off plants can be potted on, usually at liner stage.

Fog units can be preferable to mist units for weaning micropropagated plants, as the droplet size is much smaller and there is less chance of overwatering. However, carefully controlled mist, or even polythene and bottom heat, can also be used if managed well.

Micropropagation can take place all year round, which means plants such as orchids can be produced, weaned, grown on and sold all year round. Plants can be weaned from late spring onwards, but if earlier weaning is required within the production schedule, then additional lighting and heating may be required to overcome dormancy issues. However, for trees, shrubs and herbaceous perennials, the timing of the propagation also needs to take into account the dormancy period of the plants in their natural environment. Most of the hardy ornamental nursery stock propagation takes place in the spring and summer when the plant is actively growing, and the weaning takes place over winter with the plants fully weaned and ready for sale to other growers the following spring and summer.

Micropropagation is a highly skilled and technical process, so while there are kits and equipment available for the home gardener, it is unlikely to be the first type of home propagation to try!

Equipment and Materials

- Surfactants and bleach solutions.
- Laminar flow hoods.
- Sterile laboratory.
- Scalpels, tweezers.
- Test tubes and growing containers.
- Agar jelly.
- Growth hormones and nutrient solutions.
- Grow cabinets or grow rooms with suitable lighting.
- Weaning areas.

Micropropagated Plants

Many plants that would be considered difficult to propagate by traditional methods are successful using micropropagation – orchids are a prime example – but the equipment, set up and techniques are all difficult to reproduce in anything other than a commercial laboratory environment. All the plants listed in the Table are micropropagated commercially and will require the specialist equipment and treatments already discussed, though they will have differing nutrient solutions, growth hormone requirements and weaning requirements. Therefore, they are not classed as 'Easy', 'Medium' or 'Difficult' like the plant tables in the previous chapters.

Micropropagated plants

Plant
Abelia 'Edward Goucher'
Abelia grandiflora
Abelia grandiflora 'Francis Mason'
Abelia grandiflora 'Gold Spot'
Abelia schumanii
Acacia dealbata
Acer campestre cultivars
Acer capillipes cultivars
Acer cappadocicum cultivars
Acer davidii cultivars
Acer griseum cultivars
Acer japonicum cultivars
Acer negundo cultivars
Acer palmatum cultivars
Acer platanoides cultivars
Acer pseudoplatanus
Acer pseudoplatanus 'Brilliantissimum'
Actinidia kolomikta
Agapanthus africanus cultivars
Agapanthus campanulatus cultivars
Alnus cordata
Alnus glutinosa
Alnus incana
Alstroemeria cultivars
Amelanchier canadensis cultivars
Amelanchier lamarckii cultivars
Berberis thunbergii
Betula nigra cultivars
Betula pendula cultivars
Betula utilis var. *jacquemontii*
Buddleja alternifolia

Plant
Buddleja davidii cultivars
Cercis siliquastrum
Cercis siliquastrum 'Forest Pansy'
Chaenomeles × *superba* cultivars
Clematis armandii cultivars
Clematis large flowered hybrids
Clematis integrifolia cultivars
Clematis montana cultivars
Clematis viticella cultivars
Corylus avellana cultivars
Corylus maxima 'Purpurea'
Cyclamen persicum cultivars
Eucalyptus gunnii
Halesia carolina
Hebe albicans
Hebe cultivars
Hebe pimeleoides 'Quicksilver'
Hebe pinguifolia 'Pagei'
Hebe rakaiensis
Heuchera cultivars
Heucherella cultivars
Hosta cultivars
Ilex aquifolium cultivars
Ilex crenata cultivars
Ilex × *altaclerensis* cultivars
Ilex × *merserveae* cultivars
Kalmia latifolia cultivars
Lavandula angustifolia cultivars
Lavandula stoechas cultivars
Lavandula × *intermedia* cultivars
Liquidambar styraciflua cultivars

(continued overleaf)

continued

Plant
Nandina domestica cultivars
Nepeta 'Six Hills Giant'
Pachysandra terminalis cultivars
Parrotia persica
Penstemon cultivars
Phlox paniculata cultivars
Photinia × *fraseri* 'Little Red Robin'
Photinia × *fraseri* 'Pink Marble'
Photinia × *fraseri* 'Red Robin'
Potentilla fruticosa cultivars
Pulmonaria cultivars

Plant
Rhododendron cultivars
Rhododendron (deciduous azalea)
Syringa meyeri 'Palibin'
Syringa vulgaris cultivars
Taxus baccata cultivars
Tiarella cordifolia cultivars
Tiarella wherryi
Vaccinium corymbosum cultivars
Wisteria floribunda cultivars
Wisteria sinensis cultivars
Zantedeschia aethiopica 'Crowborough'

CHAPTER 14

PESTS, DISEASES AND DISORDERS

Aftercare

Many plants can be propagated successfully but then fail due to pests, disease, virus transmission, overwatering, underwatering, heat, cold, lack of light, lack of shade and myriad other reasons. This is why it is so important for the industry to have a skilled, trained workforce that sees horticulture as a career rather than a summer job. A huge amount of plant knowledge, awareness of potential issues, understanding the effects weather patterns can have on plants at different stages of growth, and all the other pest and disease knowledge is required to see a batch of plants through from propagation to sale.

Cultural Controls

A cultural control is when the process and ongoing procedures during the propagation cycle are designed to maintain the plants and the environment in a hygienic and pest-, disease- and weed-free state.

- Clean tools and preparation areas.
- High-quality stock material – pest- and disease-free.
- Propagation environment cleaned between crops.

- Regular crop inspections.
- Careful management of the environment – including water, heat and shade.
- Removal of failed propagules and debris.

Physical Controls

Physical controls can be good preventative measures:

- Traps or barriers – often these give an indication of pest activity rather than controlling them.
- Removing affected plants.
- Eradicating pests using a physical action, e.g. removing slugs.
- Netting or coverings that physically prevent a pest entering the environment.
- Weeding is important, as many pests and diseases can overwinter or start their life cycles on weeds.

Biological Controls

Biological controls are widely used in glasshouse and growing environments, and can be very effective.

They are often specific to the pest or disease, and have no harmful effect on the plant stock or wildlife. Their use needs to be timed for the control to have most effect, as they often have specific temperature and condition requirements.

- Introduction of predators or nematodes specific to the pest or disease.
- Encouraging natural predators.

Chemical Controls

Use of licensed chemicals to control and eradicate the pests or disease affecting the crop. This chapter will not specify chemicals for different pests and diseases as licences can be withdrawn, new chemicals introduced and it is, therefore, best to go directly to a horticultural supplier for the latest product.

Integrated Pest Management

Integrated pest management has become a widely used term for implementing several methods of control using four stages:

- Preventing the pests or disease.
- Identifying the pests or disease at an early stage.
- Controlling the pests or disease.
- Recording the effectiveness of each type of control used.

Once a pest or disease has been identified, integrated pest management should be implemented along the following lines:

- Physical, biological or non-chemical controls, where possible.
- Chemical controls should start with the product of least harm to other organisms, the environment and the operators.
- Chemical controls should be used at the optimum levels and frequency to reduce chemical use.
- Chemical controls should take into account the potential build up of resistance in pests.

Common Pests

It is important to use material that is pest-free, to prevent the introduction of a pest into the propagation environment; however, accidental introduction can happen. The warm and often humid atmosphere of a controlled environment can also be ideal for pests to live in. Regular inspection of the crop to ensure that early signs of pests are spotted is essential.

Aphids

There are many types of aphid that may cause damage to propagules at all stages of the production cycle. Biological controls can be very effective in controlling and eradicating them, but it is important to identify the type of aphid first, as biological controls are often specific to the species of aphid.

Damage and Symptoms of Aphids

- Aphids are sap-sucking insects that cause leaf curl and distortion.
- Stunted growth due to leaf damage.
- Sooty mould following the aphids' secretions.

Aphids on new growth of *Heuchera* cultivar.

Controls

- Cultural control – clean material, hygienic propagation areas, removal of decaying matter.
- Physical control – small infestations can be physically squashed or affected plants removed if caught early enough.
- Physical control chemicals – sprays containing surfactants that act as physical control on the aphids.
- Biological controls – parasitoid wasps or midges, which lay their eggs in the aphids. The wasp then multiplies as the eggs hatch out, increasing the numbers of predators available to parasitise the aphid population.
- Naturally occurring biological controls – hoverflies, lacewings, ladybirds and ladybird larvae.
- Chemical controls – insecticides licensed for use on aphids and the crop.

Glasshouse Whitefly

Glasshouse whitefly commonly affects crops in protected environments and can be difficult to eradicate as they thrive in the conditions that protected environments provide. However, biological controls, such as the *Encarsia formosa* wasp, are very effective. Glasshouse whitefly has a very quick life-cycle, meaning they can become detrimental to a crop very quickly.

Damage and Symptoms of Glasshouse Whitefly

- Small white, moth-like adults and scale-like immature whitefly on the underside of leaves.

Whitefly infestation starting on *Primula* cultivar.

- Stunted growth to due leaf drop.
- Leaf yellowing and lack of vigour.
- Sooty mould following the whitefly honeydew secretions.

Controls

- Cultural control – clean material, hygienic propagation areas, removal of decaying matter.
- Physical control – small infestations can be physically squashed or affected plants removed if caught early enough.
- Physical control chemicals – sprays containing surfactants that act as physical control on the whitefly.
- Biological controls – *Encarsia formosa* wasps, which lay their eggs in the aphids. The wasp then multiplies as the eggs hatch out, increasing the numbers of predators available to parasitise the aphid population. *Encarsia* will often overwinter in the protected environment.
- Chemical controls – insecticides licensed for use on whitefly and the crop.

Scale Insects

There are several species of scale insects that are problematic and the two main ones are brown scale insects and brown soft scale insects, which can affect a wide range of hosts.

Scale insects affect a wide range of plants, both in protected environments and outdoors.

Damage and Symptoms of Scale Insects

- Brown soft scale insects have flat, oval brown scales.
- Brown scale insects have more rounded, harder scales.
- Nymphs of both types are flat, creamy yellow or brown.
- Leaf yellowing and lack of vigour.
- Honeydew secretions cause sooty mould.

Controls

- Cultural control – clean material, hygienic propagation areas, removal of decaying matter.
- Physical control – leaves with small infestations can be removed from plants, affected plants removed and destroyed.
- Physical control chemicals – sprays containing surfactants that act as a physical control on the scales.
- Biological controls – nematodes can be effective on soft scale. Brown scale and scale insects with harder scale can be more difficult to control. Predatory mites that parasitize the young scale insects. Chilocorus ladybirds have some effect.
- Naturally occurring biological controls – ladybirds, lacewings.
- Chemical controls – insecticides licensed for use on scale insect and the crop.

Broad Mites

There are several species of mite that affect ornamental and food crops; broad mites are one of the most common. They are microscopic, so it is often difficult to tell which mite it is, and the symptoms can be similar to other pests.

Damage and Symptoms of Broad Mites

- Broad mites feed live on the underside of leaves.
- They feed on the growing tips and buds.
- Curling and rolling of the young leaves.
- Leaf bronzing and lack of vigour.
- Distorted growing tips.

Controls

- Cultural control – clean material, hygienic propagation areas, removal of decaying matter.
- Physical control – leaves with small infestations can be removed from plants, affected plants removed and destroyed.
- Physical control chemicals – sprays containing surfactants that act as a physical control on the mite.
- Biological controls – predatory mites that can also be used for controlling thrips and some scale insects.
- Naturally occurring biological controls – ladybirds, predatory bugs.
- Chemical controls – insecticides licensed for use on broad mites and the crop.

Two-Spotted Spider Mite

Two-spotted spider mites are a common pest but outdoors and in protected environments. The mites are small but not microscopic and can be more clearly seen in the autumn when the female turns a reddish colour. At other times the mites are green, with adults having two black spots on their backs.

Damage and Symptoms of Two-Spotted Spider Mite

- Two-spotted spider mites live on the underside of leaves.
- They feed on all parts of the leaf.
- Leaves become speckled and yellow.

Two-spotted spider mite affects a wide range of plants, usually in protected environments, and is also known as glasshouse spider mite.

- Lack of vigour.
- Webbing can be seen in severe infestations.

Controls

- Cultural control – clean material, hygienic propagation areas, removal of decaying matter.
- Physical control – leaves with small infestations can be removed from plants, affected plants removed and destroyed.
- Physical control – reducing very high temperatures and increasing humidity can reduce damage.
- Physical control chemicals – sprays containing surfactants that act as a physical control on the mite.
- Biological controls – predatory mites that can also be used for controlling thrips and some scale insects. *Neoseiulus (Amblyseius) californicus* is only licensed for use in closed environments.
- Naturally occurring biological controls – ladybirds, predatory bugs.
- Chemical controls – insecticides licensed for use on broad mites and the crop.

Mealy Bugs

There are several species of glasshouse mealy bug. New Zealand flax mealy bug is specific to phormiums and hardy enough to overwinter outside in the UK.

Damage and Symptoms of Mealy Bugs

- White, waxy and/or fluffy insects in leaf axils and around base of plants.
- Sap-sucking insects that feed on leaves, stems and sometimes roots of plants.
- Leaves become yellow and fall prematurely.
- Lack of vigour and stunted growth.
- Honeydew secretions can result in sooty mould.

Controls

- Cultural control – clean material, hygienic propagation areas, removal of decaying matter.
- Physical control – small infestations can be removed from plants, badly affected plants should be removed and destroyed.
- Physical control chemicals – sprays containing surfactants that act as a physical control on the mealy bug.

There are many species of mealy bug, some are specific to one host, the picture shows *Phormium* mealy bug, but glasshouse mealy bugs can feed on a number of host plants.

- Biological controls – predatory ladybirds and parasitic wasps that can also be used for controlling thrips and some scale insects.
- Naturally occurring biological controls – lacewing larvae.
- Chemical controls – insecticides licensed for use on mealy bugs and the crop.

Capsid Bugs

There are several species of capsid bugs that cause damage to plants, although there are also species that are predatory and beneficial. Green capsid bugs and tarnished capsid bugs are the most problematic currently in the UK.

Damage and Symptoms of Capsid Bugs

- Green adults and bright green nymphs of green capsid bugs. Brown or light green adults and green

or brown nymphs of tarnished capsid bugs. Both types are easy to see with the naked eye.
- Sap-sucking insects that cause lots of holes in leaves.
- Leaf and bud tips become distorted.
- Lack of vigour and stunted growth in badly affected plants.

Controls

- Cultural control – clean material, hygienic propagation areas, removal of decaying matter.
- Physical control – badly affected plants should be removed and destroyed.
- Physical control chemicals – sprays containing surfactants that act as a physical control on the capsid bugs and nymphs.
- Biological controls – none currently available.
- Chemical controls – insecticides licensed for use on capsid bugs and the crop.

Leaf Miners

There are many species of leaf miner, some of which are host-specific, such as the horse chestnut leaf miner; others will attack a wide range of plants.

Damage and Symptoms of Leaf Miners

- Adults are small flies that puncture the leaves causing small holes leading to necrosis.
- The larvae feed from inside the leaf and create typically wavy, pale lines in the leaf. These can then also turn necrotic.
- Leaf can become brown around the 'tunnel' created by the leaf miner, or become very pale and lace-like.
- Lack of vigour and stunted growth in badly affected plants.

Controls

- Cultural control – clean material, hygienic propagation areas, removal of decaying matter.
- Physical control – badly affected plants should be removed and destroyed.
- Physical control chemicals – sprays containing surfactants that act as a physical control on the adults.

- Biological controls – parasitic wasps can be used on some species of leaf miner for the controlling the larvae inside the leaf. Nematodes can also be effective on some species of leaf miner larvae, including the chrysanthemum leaf miner, which affects a wide range of plants other than chrysanthemums.
- Chemical controls – insecticides licensed for use on leaf miners and the crop.

Leaf Hoppers

Leaf hoppers are sap-sucking insects, generally a pale green with the ability to hop or fly short distances.

Damage and Symptoms of Leaf Hoppers

- Mottling of leaves.
- The leaves become pale and discoloured.
- Severely affected leaves look chlorotic and fall prematurely.
- Lack of vigour and stunted growth in badly affected plants.

Controls

- Cultural control – clean material, hygienic propagation areas, removal of decaying matter.
- Physical control – badly affected plants should be removed and destroyed.
- Physical control chemicals – sprays containing surfactants that act as a physical control on the nymphs and the adults.
- Biological controls – parasitic wasps can be effective if introduced early enough in the infestation.
- Chemical controls – insecticides licensed for use on leaf miners and the crop.

Sciarid Flies or Fungus Gnats

Sciarid flies are small flies, often associated with damp or overwatered conditions, particularly on houseplants and conservatory plants. The flies do not cause plant damage, but the larvae feed on roots and the base of young plant stems, so seedlings and difficult to root cuttings are vulnerable to them. They do not cause widespread damage, but are usually a sign that cultural and environmental controls may need adjusting.

Fungus gnats, or sciarid flies, can often be living in damp or wet compost.

Damage and Symptoms of Sciarid Flies

- Small flies or gnats on compost surface or flying around plants at low level.
- Damage to stems and soft tissue at the base of plants caused by the larvae.
- Lack of vigour.
- Seedlings collapsing or cuttings dying off.

Controls

- Cultural control – clean material, hygienic propagation areas, removal of decaying matter.
- Physical control – severely affected plants should be removed and destroyed.
- Physical control – ensure growing medium is freely draining and that the area is ventilated.
- Physical control chemicals – sprays containing surfactants that act as a physical control on the adults and larvae.
- Biological controls – predatory ground beetle that can also be used for the control of shore flies, which are another type of sciarid fly. Predatory mites and nematodes are also available; the nematode can be mixed in the compost during the propagation process.
- Naturally occurring biological controls – ladybirds, predatory bugs.
- Chemical controls – insecticides licensed for use on sciarid flies and the crop.

Thrips

Thrips can cause significant damage to ornamental and vegetable plants, and are particularly damaging in protected environments. Both the adults and the larvae cause damage, and the most common species is the western flower thrip. Thrips have a wide range of host plants and also transmit viruses.

Damage and Symptoms of Thrips

- Adults are pale brown flies and the larvae are oval and pale yellow.
- Adults and larvae feed on young leaves and flower bud/petals. Within the propagation cycle the damage to young leaves is more significant.
- White spots and pale patches on leaves.
- Leaves curling and distorting.

Controls

- Cultural control – clean material, hygienic propagation areas, removal of decaying matter.
- Physical control – remove affected leaves, severely affected plants should be removed and destroyed.
- Physical control chemicals – sprays containing surfactants that act as a physical control on the adults and larvae.
- Biological controls – predatory mites that feed on the larvae and can also be used for controlling scale

Thrips are tiny sap-sucking insects that can affect a range of plants.

insect and whitefly at the egg stage. Nematodes can be used as a foliar spray or mixed in the compost.

- Naturally occurring biological controls – predatory bugs, lacewings.
- Chemical controls – insecticides licensed for use on thrips and the crop.

Caterpillars

Caterpillars are not usually a significant cause of damage in propagation, but they can be a problem in outdoor beds or low tunnels. They can also cause damage during the aftercare as rooted material is being weaned or hardened off. Damage to stock plants used for propagation can also decrease the quality and amount of material available.

Damage and Symptoms of Caterpillars

- Caterpillars of varying colours and sizes on leaves.
- Moth or butterfly activity around plants.
- Damage to shoot tips and buds.
- Holes in centre of leaves.
- Holes around the edges of leaves.
- Leaves completely eaten leaving just the veins.
- Some species eat from the underside of the leaves, making transparent areas visible from the top side of the leaf.
- Leaf-rolling species roll the leaves around the growing points.
- Webbing can sometimes be seen, particularly from leaf rolling species.

Controls

- Cultural control – clean material, hygienic propagation areas, removal of decaying matter.
- Physical control – remove affected leaves, severely affected plants should be removed and destroyed.
- Physical control chemicals – sprays containing surfactants that act as a physical control.
- Biological controls – parasitic wasps, which parasitise the eggs.
- Naturally occurring biological controls – predatory ground beetles, lacewing larvae.
- Chemical controls – insecticides licensed for use on caterpillars and the crop.

Vine Weevils

Vine weevils have become a common pest both on commercial nurseries and in the domestic garden, often causing significant damage. The larvae feed on the roots of plants, often causing a complete collapse of the plant before any other symptoms appear. The adults are black beetles with pale yellow spotting. They feed on a wide range of species both ornamental and vegetable crops, and are very common in some herbaceous perennial ranges such as *Heuchera*.

Damage and Symptoms of Vine Weevils

- Characteristic notching on the edge of leaves, caused by the adults feeding. This can often be an early indication that vine weevil are present.
- Creamy coloured larvae with brown heads in growing media or soil.
- Plants wilt or collapse as roots are eaten.
- Plants lack vigour.
- Rooting occurs then plants collapse as new roots are eaten.

Controls

- Cultural control – clean material, hygienic propagation areas, removal of decaying matter.
- Physical control – remove affected plants and destroy; ensure compost is also destroyed as it may contain the larvae.
- Biological controls – nematodes can be applied as a drench to the growing medium; also effective on sciarid flies. There are different species of nematode that can be used at different times of year, depending on temperature.

Vine weevil larvae feed on the roots of a wide range of plants. The resulting damage often kills plants.

- Biological control – naturally occurring fungus that can be added to the compost. This infects and destroys the larvae, but other controls may be needed at different times of year for complete control.
- Naturally occurring biological controls – predatory ground beetles.
- Chemical controls – insecticides licensed for use on vine weevil and the crop.

Slugs and Snails

Many species of slugs live on decaying matter, but some species can cause considerable damage to both young and established plants. The conditions in a protected environment, warm and humid, are ideal for some of the most damaging species. A wide range of shrubs, herbaceous perennials and annuals are affected. Damage to stock plants can affect the quality and quantity of material available.

Damage and Symptoms of Slugs and Snails

- Slugs or snails visible on leaves.
- Slug or snail 'trails' sometimes visible – not all species leave a mucus trail.
- Holes in the middle of leaves.
- Holes around the edges of leaves.
- Tattered leaves.

Controls

- Cultural control – clean material, hygienic propagation areas, removal of decaying matter.
- Physical control – remove slugs and snails when spotted; they are often found on the underside of leaves.
- Physical control – copper-coated barriers around the propagation area.
- Biological controls – nematodes can be applied as a drench to the growing medium; also effective on slugs but not snails (the other controls listed will affect both slugs and snails). The nematode is only effective at reasonably warm soil temperatures.
- Naturally occurring biological controls – predatory ground beetles.
- Chemical controls – molluscicide licensed for use on slugs, snails and the crop.

Rodents

Germinating seedlings and young plants are attractive to rodents as a food source, particularly mice. Some seeds such as pea or sweet peas, give out pheromones that attract them at the point they are germinating. They will also eat bulbs and bulblets. Protected environments are ideal places for mice to overwinter.

Damage and Symptoms of Mice

- New shoots eaten.
- Leaves eaten and torn off.
- Seedlings and young plants dug up.
- Bulbs dug up.

Controls

- Cultural control – clean material, hygienic propagation areas, removal of decaying matter.
- Physical control – secure netting, clean areas so nesting is less likely; however, a determined mouse can get through most things.
- Physical control – traps.
- Naturally occurring controls – cats!
- Chemical controls – licensed rodent control companies can be used if the problem is serious.

Diseases

Pests and diseases often go hand in hand, and many pests cause a follow-on disease, such as sooty mould. Diseases can be easily introduced, so good hygiene and environment management are important. Protected environments often have the perfect conditions for fungal species to thrive and spread, so regular inspections are needed to spot early signs of disease. It is important to use material that is disease-free, to prevent the introduction of a disease into the propagation environment.

The most common diseases are often fungal. However, there are also bacterial diseases and oomycete diseases. Oomycete diseases are fungal-like organisms, which cause diseases such as powdery mildew and phytophthora.

Leaf Spots

Leaf spots are bacterial diseases, common in *Prunus* species, but also many other popular plants such as lavander and delphiniums.

Damage and Symptoms of Leaf Spots

- Small pale or brown spots, often irregular shapes all over the leaves.
- Spots group together and become larger.
- Spots lead to necrosis and complete holes in the leaf (shothole in *Prunus* species).
- Lack of vigour.

Controls

- Cultural control – clean material, hygienic propagation areas, removal of decaying matter.
- Cultural control – disinfect tools and equipment after each use.
- Physical control – leaves with small infestations can be removed from plants, affected plants removed and destroyed.
- Chemical controls – bactericides licensed for use on bacterial diseases and the crop.

Botrytis

Botrytis or grey mould is a common fungal disease found on a wide range of garden plants, occurring outside during the growing season and in protected environments all year round.

Damage and Symptoms of *Botrytis*

- Stems and new leaves going brown.
- Grey/brown furry appearance around the decaying stems.
- Spreads quickly between plants.
- Lack of vigour.

Controls

- Cultural control – clean material, hygienic propagation areas, removal of decaying matter.
- Cultural control – disinfect tools and equipment after each use.

- Physical control – affected plants removed and destroyed.
- Chemical controls – fungicides licensed for use on botrytis and the crop.

Powdery Mildews

Powdery mildews are a large group of fungal diseases found on a wide range of garden plants, occurring outside during the growing season and in protected environments all year round. Some are host-specific, others have a variety of hosts and they particularly occur during hot, dry weather.

Damage and Symptoms of Powdery Mildews

- White patches or spots on leaves and stems.
- Growing tips may decay or fall off.
- Spreads quickly between plants.

Controls

- Cultural control – clean material, hygienic propagation areas, removal of decaying matter.
- Cultural control – disinfect tools and equipment after each use.
- Physical control – affected plants removed and destroyed.
- Chemical controls – fungicides licensed for use on powdery mildews and the crop.

Powdery mildews are powdery white fungi that affect a wide range of host plants.

Downy Mildew

Downy mildews are a large group of fungal diseases found on a wide range of garden plants, and they can be very debilitating to the host plant. It can spread quickly through a crop resulting in failure.

Damage and Symptoms of Downy Mildews

- Yellow, brown or cream patches on leaves.
- Leaf distortion.
- Leaf drop and necrosis of leaves.
- Brown felty appearance sometimes occurs on underside of leaves.
- Spreads quickly between plants.

Controls

- Cultural control – clean material, hygienic propagation areas, removal of decaying matter.
- Cultural control – disinfect tools and equipment after each use.
- Physical control – affected plants should be removed and destroyed.
- Chemical controls – fungicides licensed for use on downy mildews and the crop.

Rusts

Rusts are another large group of fungal diseases found on a wide range of garden plants. They may be host-specific or have a variety of hosts and they can overwinter on weeds or ornamentals before flourishing during suitable conditions in the growing season.

Damage and Symptoms of Rusts

- Yellow, brown, white or orange pustules on leaves and stems – they come many colours.
- Leaves can curl and become distorted.
- Spreads quickly between plants.

Controls

- Cultural control – clean material, hygienic propagation areas, removal of decaying matter.
- Cultural control – disinfect tools and equipment after each use.
- Physical control – affected plants should be removed and destroyed,
- Chemical controls – fungicides licensed for use on rusts and the crop.

Damping Off

Damping off affects seedlings both before germination and after. It is caused by a wide range of fungal species.

Damage and Symptoms of Damping Off

- Seedlings fail to germinate.
- Seedlings collapse, often in circular groups.
- White mould appears on and around seedlings.

Downy mildew causes mouldy patches on plant leaves, and is often associated with wet conditions.

Damping off is caused by propagation conditions being too wet, poorly ventilated and overcrowding of seedlings.

Controls

- Cultural control – clean material, hygienic propagation areas, removal of decaying matter.
- Cultural control – disinfect tools and equipment after each use.
- Cultural control – ensure seeds are not sown as thinly as possible.
- Cultural control – avoid overwatering and ensure good ventilation.
- Physical control – affected plants removed and destroyed.
- Chemical controls – fungicides licensed for use on damping off and the crop.

Black Leg or Stem Rots

Black leg is associated with pelargoniums and geraniums, and other stem rots can often occur in the rooting environment. The controls for this are mainly cultural, and avoidance and prevention are easier than trying to treat the problem.

Damage and Symptoms of Black Leg or Stem Rots

- Blackening of the stems, sometimes toward the base.
- Stems browning and becoming very soft.
- Cuttings collapse.

Controls

- Cultural control – clean material, hygienic propagation areas, removal of decaying matter.
- Cultural control – disinfect tools and equipment after each use.
- Cultural control – ensure cuttings are from healthy stock.
- Cultural control – avoid overwatering and ensure good ventilation.
- Physical control – affected plants should be removed and destroyed.
- Chemical controls – fungicides licensed for use on stem rots and the crop.

Disorders

Disorders can have a wide range of effects on propagated material, and are caused by changes in the protected environment, rather than a pest or disease. However, it is important to observe the links between disorders caused by changes in the environment and the potential follow on of pests and diseases. All three are interlinked, which is why good crop management is essential.

Excessive Light Levels

Excessive light levels during the growing season appear to be becoming more common. They can happen very quickly, with the light levels increasing rapidly over a few hours.

Damage and Symptoms of Excessive Light Levels

- Leaves become pale.
- New growth becomes scorched and yellow or pale.
- Leaves drop prematurely.

Controls

- Cultural control – plants going from shading to higher light levels should be monitored.
- Physical control – shading applied before light levels increase in intensity.
- Physical control – dieback should be pruned off affected plants.

Leaf Scorch

Leaf scorch can also be caused by overhead watering during the growing season, when temperatures and light levels are high.

Damage and Symptoms of Leaf Scorch

- Leaf spots occur where the water droplets touched them.
- Brown scorching around the edges of the leaves.
- Leaves drop prematurely.

Controls

- Cultural control – increase shading if overhead watering needs to take place during hot periods.
- Cultural control – reduce droplet size of overhead watering, if possible.

Leaf scorch can happen if shade net isn't used in strong sunlight conditions.

- Cultural control – do not use overhead watering during the hottest part of the day.

Cold Temperatures

Newly propagated plants are vulnerable to drops in temperature, regardless of how hardy the parent plant is. Fluctuating temperatures, when plants do not have time to become acclimatized, can cause considerable damage.

Damage and Symptoms of Cold Temperatures

- New growth and growing tips brown or blacken.
- Brown scorching around the edges of the leaves.
- Leaves drop prematurely.
- Root death.

Controls

- Cultural control – check minimum temperatures and increase protection during cold periods.
- Cultural control – maintain stable temperatures to avoid fluctuations.
- Physical control – prune back damaged plants.
- Physical control – remove and destroy badly affected plants.

Overwatering

Overwatering is a common cause of failure in both vegetative propagation and seed germination. The young propagules do not have roots, or enough roots once they have rooted, to take up excess water.

Damage and Symptoms of Overwatering

- New growth becomes pale and chlorotic.
- Roots don't develop on cuttings.
- Seedlings damp off.
- Developed roots rot off.
- Root death.

Controls

- Cultural control – check growing media for signs of overwatering and poor drainage.
- Cultural control – reduce watering.
- Cultural control – increase bottom heat for a short period to reduce excess water.
- Physical control – remove and dispose of affected plants.

INDEX

aftercare   35, 52, 65, 77, 86, 93, 98, 102, 115, 131
air layering   96
asexual plant reproduction   12

biological controls   27, 131–132
bulb propagation   119–123

chemical controls   27, 132
chip budding   113–114
compound layering   96–97
conifers   11
cross-pollination   8
cultural controls   131

diseases
    black leg or stem rots   142
    botrytis   140
    damping off   141
    downy mildews   141
    leaf spots   140
    powdery mildews   140
    rusts   141
disorders
    cold temperatures   143
    excessive light levels   142
    leaf scorch   142
    overwatering   143
division   101–105

environmental factors   12–13
environments and materials
    fogging units   19
    growing media   20–23
    hoops and polythene   19–20
    humidity   18
    light and shading   17–18
    low tunnels   20
    mist systems   18–19
    sun tunnels   20
    tools and equipments   24–26

fertilization   9
flower parts   9–10

grafting and budding   107–117

hardwood cuttings   75–81
hormone-rooting agents   27

integrated pest management   132
    aphids   132–133

broad mites   134
capsid bugs   135–136
caterpillars   138
glasshouse whitefly   133
leaf hoppers   136
leaf miners   136
mealy bugs   135
rodents   139
scale insects   133–134
sciarid flies   136–137
slugs and snails   139
thrips   137–138
two-spotted spider mites   134–135
vine weevils   138–139

layering   95–99
leaf-bud cuttings   89–93
leaf, leaf-section and petiole cuttings   93–97

micropropagation   125–129
modified stem propagation techniques   121–122
mound layering or stooling   95

oomycete diseases   139

physical controls   131
plant propagation   7
pollination   8
propagation
    advantages and disadvantages   13–15
    environmental factors   12

root cuttings   83–87

seed sowing   29–45
semi-ripe cuttings   61–73
serpentine layering   96, 97
sexual plant reproduction   8
    in flowering plants   9–10
    flower parts   10
    in non-flowering plants   11
side veneer graft   112–113
simple layering   95
softwood cuttings   47–59

vegetative propagation   12

whip and tongue graft   110–111
whip or splice graft   108–109